Software by Design

Creating People Friendly Software for the Macintosh

Software by Design

Creating People Friendly Software
for the Macintosh

Penny Bauersfeld

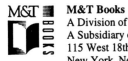 **M&T Books**
A Division of MIS:Press
A Subsidiary of Henry Holt and Company, Inc.
115 West 18th Street
New York, New York 10011

Limits of Liability and Disclaimer of Warranty
The Author and Publisher of this book have used their best efforts in preparing the book and the programs contained in it. These efforts include the development, research, and testing of the theories and programs to determine their effectiveness.

The Author and Publisher make no warranty of any kind, expressed or implied, with regard to these programs or the documentation contained in this book. The Author and Publisher shall not be liable in any event for incidental or consequential damages in connection with, or arising out of, the furnishing, performance, or use of these programs.

```
Bauersfeld, Penny
Software by design : creating people friendly software for the
Macintosh / Penny Bauersfeld
        p.       cm.
Includes index.
ISBN 1-55828-296-3 : $29.95
        1. Macintosh (Computer)--Programming. 2. Computer software-
-Development.  3. User-computer interaction.  I Title.
QA76.8.M3B375  1994
005.265--dc20
                                        93-46242
                                           CIP
```

Trademarks
Throughout this book, trademarked names are used. Rather than put a trademark symbol after every occurance of a trademarked name, we used the names in an editorial fashion only, and to the benefit of the trademark owner, with no intention of infringement of the trademark. Where such designations appear in this book, they have been printed with initial caps.

Publisher: Steve Berkowitz
Associate Publisher: Brenda McLaughlin
Development Editor: Margot Pagan
Production Editor: Mark Masuelli
Associate Production Editor: Joseph McPartland

Copy Editor: Jeri Marler
Technical Editor: Ed Hogan
Illustrations: Jean Ann Greaves,
Joseph McPartland, Penny Bauersfeld

97   96   95   94   4   3   2   1

For Poppy

Table of Contents

Chapter 5: On-line Tools and Procedures 109

Chapter 7: Usability Testing 193

Chapter 8: Iteration 245

Chapter 9: Applying the User-Oriented Design Process..................................281

Chapter 10: Extending the User-Oriented Design Process..................................295

Acknowledgements

The process described in this book has evolved over the years from work I have completed with many of my colleagues. In particular, I would like to thank Kathleen Gomoll for sharing her skills and secrets for working with people, and Laurie Vertelney for her endless creativity and design ideas. Thanks to Tony Meadow for your confidence and guidance; Margot Owens Pagan, Mark Masuelli, Jules Gilder and others at MIS/M&T for making this happen; and my family and friends who supported and encouraged me and gave me the time and energy to write this book.

Preface

Most software user interfaces are designed by programmers and, unfortunately, it shows. Most programmers have had no training in interface design. Programmers are trained to work with computers, but not with people. Most of us programmers have learned something of user interface design the hard way, but there is a lot that we just don't know.

Computer users are more and more demanding. The largest software companies have all established interface design groups and many of them have produced higher quality applications. Consequently, users expect all applications to rise to these higher standards, including those from medium and small-sized companies. High quality user interfaces are expected of all applications.

As a programmer you know too much and yet not enough to design great user interfaces. You know far more than most of your users about what happens within the computer (unless you're creating a developer tool). On the other hand, you might have forgotten most of what it was like using a computer to accomplish day-to-day tasks.

This book will help you produce high quality interfaces that are easy to learn and easy to use. Penny Bauersfeld explains clearly and concisely the techniques which you can use to design, evaluate and test user interfaces. She also gives you tips, tricks and things to avoid when doing interface design, some of which are not readily described.

In this book you'll learn about how to go about designing user interfaces, no matter what development tool you are using. It shouldn't matter to your users that you've used C++ or Omnis or any other tool. What matters to them is that your software helps them accomplish their tasks and goals.

The techniques and processes described in this book are not specific to the Macintosh, or, in fact, even to computers. What you learn from this book is applicable to developing applications under IBM's Presentation Manager or Microsoft Windows or any other interface.

I'll be looking for more applications with better interfaces.

Anthony Meadow

Why This Book is for You

If you're the head of a program design team or a programmer determined to design software that people can successfully use, this book is for you. If you are a medium to small-sized company competing with major software companies with established interface design groups, this book will be of invaluable help to you in your efforts to design better user interfaces.

Or, if you are already in the process of designing user interfaces and aren't sure how to proceed, this book with its techniques, tips and tricks - and common pitfalls - can save you hours of effort and enhance your on-going pursuit of better user interfaces.

Software By Design: Designing People-Friendly Software takes you through the design process step-by-step, with a progressive exercise called the "Supermarket Example", which provides opportunity for the user to try out each of the techniques in a real world problem. When the user completes the exercises, at the end of the book he will have practiced the design methods to create a completed user interface design. A design that the reader has constructed along the way with advice and guidance from the author, Penny Bauersfeld.

1

From understanding "the art of evaluating what people currently do and how technology can improve the process;" to learning new techniques that can expand user interface design skills; to using and evaluating user studies; to off- and on-line tools and procedures, Software By Design: Designing People-Friendly Software covers it all—and more. Prototyping, usability testing, iteration, and the extending and application of the user interface design process are discussed and illustrated.

The book itself is oriented toward its users, the readers—the informative and intuitive narration deals with both the simpler aspects of design construction, graduating, comfortably, into more sophisticated areas of user interface design.

Introduction

Software development typically follows the technological advancements of the hardware on which it runs. A software engineering team determines the functionality of the computer, then writes a software application that accesses the hardware features. However, the person who uses the software has tasks in mind, not the workings of a computer.

Successful software developers separate the technology from the interaction. The people who use their software think of the computer as an aid in accomplishing tasks rather than as an obstacle.

The real trick is to design software based on users' needs, then to map this functionality to the underlying hardware, rather than the other way around. The primary goal of any system should be to do what users need, rather than getting it to work bug-free. The system will be bug-free eventually, but this should be a secondary goal.

User needs and opinions should be an integral part of software design. To identify the functionality and interaction that will make the user's task as straightforward as possible, find out what users want. Watch them at work.

3

Listen to what they say about what they do and would like to do. Then use what you have learned as you develop the system.

Amazingly enough, users are often the last to be consulted about a software product, if they are asked at all! For many software developers, user testing is applied after the software is fully designed, and typically it is done only to identify bugs. It is more appropriate to consult with users early on so that their input can really help the development team to build better software.

This book presents a user-interface design process oriented toward users. It introduces various methods and techniques for involving users, and provides examples of software systems built by applying these methodologies. It is a guide to an approach for designing software systems rather than a complete how-to instruction. Development of individual user interfaces is dependent on a number of factors not addressed in this text, including: screen layout and principles of graphic design, correct wording of text, and internationalization of the user interface. The specifics of user-interface development are discussed in other sources, and therefore are only introduced in this book. Instead, the focus is on methodologies not widely published as approaches to user interface design. You will learn that by involving users in the various phases of design, you can develop creative, dynamic, and functional systems.

This book is a result of my many years of experience developing interactive graphical software for Macintosh systems. The examples and exercises in the book draw primarily from Macintosh software. While the process is tried and true for Macintosh software, it is relevant for any hardware platform.

How this Book is Structured

This book presents techniques for designing computer software. These techniques are organized in units according to their general roles in the design process.

Chapter 1 discusses the user-oriented design process; how to identify users and take advantage of their input and expertise; the role of an interdisciplinary design team in user interface design; the importance of visual design; and how to apply software skills.

Chapter 2 presents a user-interface design exercise that is the subject of a series of tasks throughout the technique sections. The importance of completing the tasks is also discussed.

Chapters 3-8 present the components and techniques of the user-oriented design process. Each chapter has an introductory section describing that part in the design process. Other sections discuss the techniques, which are accompanied by tasks to complete for the exercise.

Chapter 9 discusses how to apply the various elements of this process to your own design problems, including: how to integrate the techniques into your existing design process, how to attain the necessary support from your organization for putting this process to work, and how to identify which parts of the process to use in your own problems.

Chapter 10 explores ways to customize the process by adding techniques of your own or elaborating on some of the techniques presented.

Chapter 1

An Approach to User-Oriented Interface Design

The User and the Task

When you invite guests to dinner, you plan the menu to suit their culinary preferences. You may have a new rotisserie that cooks a delicious roast, but if your guests are vegetarians, you wouldn't think of serving them beef. Your ice-cream maker may churn out the best toasted-almond variety you've ever tasted, but if your guests are lactose intolerant, you wouldn't serve them a creamy dairy dessert.

Why, then, do software developers present users with applications fraught with complex, technology-dependent features? Just because a machine can do something doesn't mean people want the machine to do that something. People want software that does what they need, when they need it—not software that does what it can. If software developers would ask people who use their software what they want, software would meet the needs of the people who use it.

7

If asking users what they want were a well understood task, everyone would be doing it. There is an art to evaluating what people currently do and understanding how technology can improve the process. Still, there are a number of techniques that can help even the novice to understand user needs. Once users are engaged, goals for the technology become clear. Understanding these goals helps system designers to identify and design tasks that are the key to a successful user interface design.

User-oriented software design principles are akin to product design principles for products of all kinds (not just software). These principles are also related to the evolution of human concerns in software design via the field of human factors. Understanding the foundations of user-oriented design is important to interpreting its purpose and application. However, user-oriented design principles alone do not ensure successful software. Other strategies and skills are important as well: use of an interdisciplinary design team, applying sound visual design principles, and having solid software implementation skills wherever possible. These strategies and skills are presented in this chapter, but are not covered in depth. By incorporating them in a user-oriented approach to system design, software developers can focus on delivering clear, useful systems that meet user needs.

Addressing the User in Product Design

In the world of product design, whole fields of discipline and degree programs at universities are devoted to addressing user needs. Industrial and product design professionals ensure that products such as appliances, automobiles, and furniture conform to the needs of the people using them. Industrial designers realize that if their products are not useful, the products' beauty and elegance are unimportant. Software designers can learn much from the experience of product and industrial designers, and by studying the products they design.

Figure 1.1 Product design with users in mind. This coffee pot is an example of a consumer product designed with its users in mind. The handles of both the coffee carafe and the filter cup are easily accessible and fit snugly in an adult's hand. The clear glass of the carafe with the written measures on the side make it easy to first measure water to pour into the machine and then see how much coffee is ready. The latch on the bottom of the filter cup allows the user to pull out the carafe while the coffee is brewing without spilling coffee onto the burner below. Overall, the design is straightforward and easy to interpret.

In the early days of computing, because software was not thought of as a separate product, hardware designers were responsible for making usable software products. Yesterday's hardware designers are today's human factors professionals (more on this later). Software engineering has evolved from the general field of computer engineering. With the separation of application software from machine or system software, today's software designers must be concerned with product design. Software developers must think of their products on the same level as other products such as appliances and automobiles. Realizing that they have individual products with specific marketing needs, software development companies have been quick to address the business side of the product world by adding sales and marketing staff. However, it is time software development companies address the needs of people who use their software by involving a team of designers who contribute early and throughout all stages of the development. Assessing and addressing the needs of users during the design process will guarantee successful, people-oriented software products.

Human Factors versus User-Oriented Design

While software designers have been slow to apply principles of product design, the field of computing has not been totally without concern for its human users. Human factors experts are concerned with addressing the equipment needs of users. Typically, they focus on the ergonomics of computers, and address issues such as: Can the user adequately perceive data on the computer screen? Can the user access the keys on the keyboard? Ergonomic concerns are certainly important to the success of computer hardware, but the application of ergonomic concerns to software design is less clear. It is important to ask questions like these: Can the user distinguish elements on the screen? Can the user select those elements with the mouse? However, software designers concentrating on user-oriented design are concerned with more than ergonomics.

The field of human/computer interaction grew out of the first meeting of human factors specialists, held in 1982 in Gaithersburg, Maryland. This special topics session of the Association of Computing Machinery (ACM) served as the foundation for the ACM Special Interest Group of Computer–Human Interaction (SIGCHI). SIGCHI has evolved into an organization that addresses many concerns of software and hardware developers who focus on the human-oriented aspects of computing. Although human factors is only one area addressed by the professionals who make up SIGCHI, the name of ACM's annual SIGCHI conference publication is "Human Factors in Computing Systems." The field of human factors is, in fact, very different from user-oriented design.

Figure 1.2 ACM SIGCHI materials. The Association for Computing Machinery's Special Interest Group on Computer-Human Interaction puts out a number of publications for user interface professionals. These include the proceedings of the annual SIGCHI conferences and a quarterly journal, both of which publish relevant articles and papers of interest to user interface designers.

So how does user-oriented design differ from human factors work? As noted previously, human factors professionals make sure the physical needs of human users are met. Usability testing, an important part of user-oriented design, has probably grown in large part from the work of human factors experts. User-oriented design goes beyond physical concerns to involve the user in a range of different ways at all stages of the design process. Involving the user is not simply making sure the user can adequately see, comprehend, or use something, although these important concerns should certainly be addressed by software developers. The added benefits of user-oriented design are in product usability and the creative designs that build on user concerns and needs. It involves the user to direct the design of a product–to choose the metaphors on which a software model is based, or the visual elements that will present certain product concepts. User-oriented design is a way of thinking about software design, not simply principles applied at a specific point in the design process. It can help solve design problems, or provide direction for developers choosing among various approaches.

Different designs involve different user-oriented concerns. Understanding what these concerns are and when they should be addressed is both a science and an art. Sound user-oriented design experience is attained over time. The following chapters present user-oriented design principles and concerns with an exercise designed to help you put the principles into practice. Applying the principles to your own work and experiences should make evident the creative process of user-oriented design and the many ways it can address user needs.

Interdisciplinary Design

In many traditional software development environments, software engineers are responsible for building the software. Their process typically includes: designing the software; designing the way the system will look and function; designing the code to get the system to work; and spending long hours coding and debugging the actual system. When I was trained as a software engineer, my professors spent hours lecturing on the writing and debugging of programs and code, but relatively little time discussing system design and functionality, or explaining principles for interactive graphical user interface design. The discipline of software engineering prepares students for designing and writing the code, but the user interface is often an afterthought. Sometimes a single course—or worse, a single lecture—is devoted to principles of user interface design. Programs devoted to user interface design are beginning to appear in some select universities, but these programs are few and limited. As a result, user interface principles are taught to only a minority of software engineers.

This is not necessarily bad news for user interface design. Software engineers are trained to write programs and get them working—extremely valuable skills for systems development. However, they are not necessarily the people who should design what the systems do or how they appear to users. If they do design these systems, they should follow a process that meets the needs of the users, rather than one designed solely to implement the system. They should work with experts who are trained to interpret user needs and determine system functionality accordingly, and with experts in graphic and screen design. Together, the software engineer, the designer, and the user expert can form an interdisciplinary team that will meet many needs of the system.

There are a number of advantages to an interdisciplinary team approach to software design. The most obvious is that multiple concerns are addressed simultaneously throughout development. Additionally, team members can devote their energies to their area of expertise, and work together with other members to ensure the smooth integration of all the parts of the design. When a user advocate, who is in contact with users throughout the design process, presents user needs and concerns at team meetings and development sessions, then the user is represented at all stages. The graphic or industrial designer can generate quick sketches to show users for testing purposes, and to show engineers to ensure that the front-end design and the implementation are synchronized. While it may seem more costly, in the long run having an interdisciplinary team saves time and resources in development because skills are available when they are needed. Software design is not just about implementing software, and the majority of team resources should not be devoted to programming. Good software design requires a balance of many skills; devoting time to design with interdisciplinary team members will save programming time later.

Figure 1.3 An interdisciplinary team working together.
One of the most effective tools for user interface design is the inter-disciplinary team. Team members contribute skills from various disciplines, including (as represented here) Visual design, Psychology and Computer Science.

The most important contribution of an interdisciplinary team is that ultimately user needs are met in the software development process. The design team continually evaluates whether the needs of the user are being met, not simply whether or not the software is functional. In the long run, the software is more interesting and robust because development team members represent varied disciplines. Having someone like a film production expert for a video product, or a musician for a sound product, leads to more innovative products that present functionality in unique and exciting ways.

The composition of a specific team depends on the nature of the software being developed and the budget of the project, which ultimately determines the number of people the team can support. Some obvious team candidates are experts in computer science, psychology, and graphic arts. A team of three people with a representative from each of these fields can probably ensure that programming, user, and design needs are met. Some other fields to draw from are:

Cognitive science. Cognitive scientists are generally computer scientists trained in the patterns of human cognition and how that can be translated to computing. Cognitive scientists might be useful in developing artificial intelligence software, or software that models human thought processes.

Industrial design. Industrial designers are traditionally trained in product design, with a focus on hardware or packaging concerns. They might be particularly helpful with products that rely heavily on hardware interactivity (in addition to or instead of software), or with consumer products based on human interaction with physical components.

Anthropology. Anthropologists are trained to observe human behavior and interaction; they often study the way people perform certain tasks or behave in certain environments or cultures. An anthropologist might be useful on a team exploring the ramifications of a new technology for user interface, or one where the technology will dramatically change the work practices of the group who will use it.

Sociology. Like psychologists, sociologists study human behavior, but they specialize in group interaction. A sociology expert might be a critical member on a team developing software for group work, or academic software designed to be used by numerous people simultaneously.

Film/video production. Film and video production professionals use media to communicate stories or messages. As the boundary between computer and television dissolves, computer software must meet the entertainment needs of a generation weaned on MTV. These skills will become increasingly important to software development teams.

Sound. As computing sound technologies advance and merge with analog sound production systems, high-quality sound is increasingly important in computer software design. For software that requires high-quality sound, a sound expert (a musician and/or technician) becomes a critical contributor to the development team.

Entertainment. Entertainment experts trained in attendance trends are becoming more prominent as our society continues to merge work and leisure. Having an entertainment expert on an interdisciplinary-software design team could help make a piece of software more compelling than a competitor's product.

The ultimate goal for an interdisciplinary team is to work together to map user needs onto a functional product. If project constraints make it impossible to include multiple experts on the team, it still helps to identify the necessary roles and have one person "wear different hats" when the need arises. Another alternative is to bring in experts as consultants during critical development phases. Even a few hours with someone skilled in another discipline is better than no interdisciplinary input at all. You must do whatever you can within the constraints of your project to solicit input from multiple disciplinarians in your software development process. Recognizing the need for this is the crucial first step in interdisciplinary design.

Visual Design

One of the most important elements of a Graphical User Interface (GUI) is the visual design. Sometimes referred to as screen or graphic design, it is critical in communicating information to, and interacting with, users. The success of systems similar to the Macintosh, which rely heavily on pleasing aesthetics, demonstrates that the benefits of good visual design are well supported by user interface designers. Strong visual design alone does not necessarily ensure a user interface that meets user needs. It does mean, however, that when user input is provided, it can be adequately and pleasingly communicated.

Although they have slightly different meanings, the terms graphic design and visual design are often used interchangeably when applied to computer user interfaces. Graphic design refers to basic layout and form principles of text, patterns, and illustrations, originally developed for traditional media such as paper imagery. Visual design is more comprehensive because it concerns all the visual elements of the software: text, still images, illustrations, animation, photographic images, video, and the visual representation of the non-graphic components such as sound or speech.

These basic principles of graphic design have been updated to address GUI concerns: form and separation of space; text size and legibility; integration of text and graphics; and the use of color. New principles have been developed specifically for computer screen design. There are now a number of textbooks and seminars on the topic of graphic design for computer user interfaces. Years ago there was a shortage of experts skilled in computer software visual design and few tools with which to work. Today you can find many specialists and tools.

Many computer graphic design professionals are also skilled in multimedia formats such as video, animation, and other forms of computer art. They are experienced with advanced paint or video production software, as well as with hardware such as pen-based input devices and color scanners.

Sometimes software developers enlist the services of graphic specialists to design icons or complete other small graphic details. However, visual design is more than icon design or finishing graphical touches. While involving graphic designers at the end of the design cycle is a step in the right direction, it does not address larger visual design concerns. Successful visual design typically involves experts throughout the process—from the early conceptual stage that influences the structure of the software, to the details of the icons and dialog boxes.

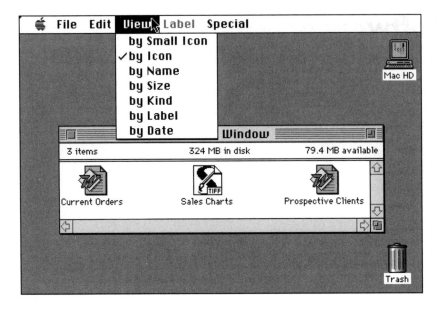

Figure 1.4 Visual elements of the Macintosh screen.
The Macintosh desktop user interface is made up of a number of
components where visual representation plays a significant role
in the effectiveness of both functionality and interaction. The clearly
distinct layout of various elements, with the menu bar across the
top, icons on the right side (at least initially) and windows open
in the central desktop area help users to locate and differentiate
interface elements and functions. The visual language of various
aspects such as window details, icon rendering and font clarity
are also important in communicating purpose to users. Though it
cannot be represented here in a single screen representation of
the Mac desktop, visual detail also plays an important role in
interactive feedback. While not all user interfaces should follow
the exact features or representation style of the Macintosh desktop, they stand to learn from the clear graphic design principles
applied here.

Software Implementation Skills

It is important not to overstate the need for design and user skills to a point where implementation skills seem unimportant. Clearly, without the ability to implement a system that is designed to meet user needs, all the user research we do is useless. A successful software design team should be able to understand user needs, design the system, and then put the system in place.

Quality software engineers must possess a variety of skills in order to: analyze system requirements; determine how best to interface with the operating system; develop the algorithms necessary to support required functionality; and finally to get the system working. The importance of skilled software engineers is unquestioned. My hope is that the user-oriented focus of this book will help software engineers to problem solve specifically to meet user needs. Rather than compromise user needs for the sake of the software, strong software engineers can adapt their designs to better support users.

Chapter 2

The Exercise

L earning new techniques helps to expand user interface design skills. Putting those techniques into practice is an important way to see their value and understand how best to use them. It would be ideal if you had a user interface design problem to solve while learning the techniques in this book. Having a real-life problem to solve with these methods would provide additional motivation for learning and applying the different techniques.

Because it is unlikely you have such a software project waiting to be developed, this book includes an exercise to help you take advantage of the methods introduced in Chapters 3 through 8. Although it is not necessarily the type of design problem you will solve in your own work, it provides hands-on experience to help you learn. Following each technique section is a task requiring you to use the technique. Complete all the tasks and you will have accomplished the exercise. If you choose not to do the tasks, just reading about them will help you understand how to apply the techniques to a real design problem. If you do complete the tasks, you will have a head start on using the techniques when you apply them to your problems. You will have a clearer understanding of their roles and advantages. Refer to Chapters 3 through 8 when you apply techniques to your design projects, to help you focus on your goals and intentions.

The Supermarket Guide Exercise

The exercise that will illustrate the techniques for user-oriented software design is to develop an on-line supermarket guide. Think of the guide as a central information station for the supermarket. It might provide information about the supermarket itself, the products it stocks, pricing information, customer purchasing trends, or all of the above. It might be used by supermarket employees, customers, or other involved parties. It is up to you to decide the scope and functionality of your application, and to target the user population for the supermarket guide.

You are free to set the objectives for—and define the constraints of—the guide. In this way, you can tailor the guide to be relevant to your own work. For instance, if you develop networking software, you might want to design the guide to be a networked application linking many supermarkets. If you develop portable device software, you might want to develop a portable supermarket guide. The possibilities are endless. There are no right or wrong solutions to this exercise—it is what you make of it. Remember, the intent is to give you hands-on experience with the techniques presented in the book, not to actually build a supermarket guide!

Questions to consider before you begin the techniques exercise include:

Where will the guide be located?
It might be stationed in the supermarket, available to customers at home, portable (so it can be at home or at the market or wherever the user goes!), or some other specific site. You might want to complete some early user research first (see Chapter 3) to help you decide where the guide will be, or

you might simply want to dictate the location and make it a constraint of your design.

How many guides will there be?

Are you designing a single guide to be placed in one supermarket, or will it be accessible from every branch of the chain? Will it be available at the supermarket and remotely from home? If there will be more than one guide, will they be standalone units or will they be networked?

What kind of hardware platform will be needed?

Are there hardware elements you know you want to incorporate, or will you determine the hardware needs based on your user studies (Chapter 3) and early designs (Chapter 4)? Will there be a screen display, and thus a graphic component? What input device will you use—keyboard, touch screen, track ball, or voice input (possibly via a phone receiver)? Will the guide use sound or video?

Is size a factor?

What are the physical constraints of the guide? Think about where the guide will go, and how big or small it could reasonably be.

Is cost a factor?

Are you on a limited budget? (For the purposes of this exercise, you have no actual budget. In real life it will be rare to have a design project that is not cost constrained in some way.) Cost constraints might affect the hardware platform you elect to use, or the total development time. If cost constraints are typical of your work, you should apply some here to help you design in a situation more realistic to your own.

Who are the users?

You might want to wait to decide who the actual users are until after you've done some early user studies (Chapter 3), or you might want to decide this now to help you focus your design work. Potential users include supermarket employees, customers, check-out clerks, or subsets or supersets of these groups. You might decide on a completely different target user population.

What type of information will be provided?

Again, this question might be answered with early user research (Chapter 3) or designs (Chapter 4), or you might want to make these decisions now. Knowing your user group will help determine the contents of the guide.

Is it customizable?

Will the guide be adaptable to either the location or the person using it? If so, what are the implications for your design?

Will it need to be updated?

Is the information in the guide entered only once and intended to remain static over the life of the guide? Or must it be updated on a regular basis—daily, weekly, monthly, annually, or some other interval? If you want to update information, how will you enter new data—by floppy disk, across a network, or some other means?

Is it tied to other supermarket functions?

Since the guide is a computerized system, you might want to take advantage of, or incorporate other, computerized systems currently in the supermarket. Some candidates might be check-out functions, coupon distribution or gathering, or even remote home delivery. If these functionalities don't exist at the candidate supermarket, consider the possibility that they will eventually, and design the guide so it can be tied into these functions in the future.

You might not address all of these issues before you begin the first tasks, but thinking about them will help to direct your design. Answers to these questions might come from the early exercises in user studies and research. Tailor your early user studies to gather information appropriate to your design problem. If you have concerns in your real work that would lead you to put design constraints on the exercise, by all means do so.

Substituting Another Exercise Topic

The supermarket guide was chosen for this exercise because most people can relate to it. User research for the guide is easily accessible to anyone who frequents a supermarket, and the possibilities are endless for tailoring a supermarket guide to your own special concerns. Some readers, however, might feel they have enough real problems and don't want to spend time designing a supermarket guide they will never use.

If you are adverse to the supermarket guide, feel free to substitute another exercise problem. Remember, the purpose of the exercise is not so that all readers can design automated information systems for supermarkets across the country. It is to provide experience with the design techniques as you learn about them. Better to substitute another design problem for the supermarket guide than to ignore the exercise.

Importance of Applied Design

The best way to learn the techniques is to do them. The best way to do them is to apply them to a real-world problem. Having a single design problem that progresses as you learn will help you see the relationship among the techniques and how they work. This will be true not only in the supermarket guide problem, but in later user interface design, as well.

By trying out these techniques, as you read about them, you will have a reference point in later design problems. You might forget the relevance of the methods or the way they are related if you do not practice applying them to a design problem. When you are faced with real problems in your own work, you will be able to turn to the examples and prototypes you created in completing this exercise and remember how you applied this methodology before.

You might want to create a team (possibly with other readers) to work on the exercise. By working as a team (interdisciplinary, if possible), sharing the experience, and learning together you could create a greater design. If you are fortunate enough to work with others as a team, your experience will be richer.

The Exercise Tasks

A task is presented at the end of each technique section in Chapters 3 through 8. If you choose not to complete the task, at least read about it so you understand more about applying the technique to real-world problems.

Making it Work for You

Not every technique included in this book is appropriate for every design problem. You might want to choose only those that make sense for your design. Some of these tasks lend themselves more to the supermarket guide than to other problems. However, if you practice all the techniques found here, you will be better able to choose those appropriate to your real-world design projects, and it might even save you time later. With experience, you will understand which techniques make sense for your specific design problems, and practicing them now will help you understand how to apply them.

Chapter 3

Early User Studies

What are Early User Studies?

Before the actual implementation of a project, you should consider conducting research to help direct the design and development process. Research involving potential users can be critical to identifying the goals of the system and the tasks it should perform. User research can take a number of forms and involve many different types of resources. The actual time spent on user research varies according to what is known about users and the system, the schedule of the project, and the resources available to dedicate to user research. All the user research that occurs early in the project cycle, often before any other work is started, can be thought of as early user studies.

User studies are just what they sound like—studies of users. In addition to the potential users of the system being designed, studies might include alternative user groups. These are not tests because they are rarely formal evaluations of a system in use (as are usability tests done later in the product design cycle). The studies might involve observation of people at work, interviews with users or other experts in the field, task analysis to identify what users are doing, or studies in which the user gathers information over time (called seed studies).

The unifying characteristic of all user studies is that they help designers understand more about the potential system through the people who will use it. User studies conducted before design begins impart important knowledge about the system that might otherwise be overlooked. They can support designs, or point out what is missing from a current design. They ensure that system development is driven by what users need rather than what the technology can provide.

The various methods of user studies presented in the following sections are not meant to be exhaustive. They are a foundation to help you understand their value. I encourage you to develop new user study methods for your circumstances.

The Advantages of Early User Studies

Early user studies can support the software development process in a number of ways. When appropriately structured and conducted, user studies will:

Help to identify system functionality.
Observing users while they perform a task clarifies the critical elements or steps in that task. For instance, if most users use certain features and ignore others, the desired system functionality becomes clear. Looking at the system solely for evaluation purposes cannot provide the same feedback as seeing what users actually do.

Introduce design ideas.
Analyzing the ways users approach their tasks, or talking with users about how they might approach a task using alternative technology, might intro-

duce ideas for a new product. Users are the direct beneficiaries of new products and technologies. They can provide critical direction on design options, both in terms of features and actual implementation details.

Test technology capabilities.
Users often think that new technologies in the work place are particularly disruptive. By placing prototypes in the target work area, you can observe whether the technology supports the desired tasks. Evaluating and refining the system with prototypes means the transition to the new system can be a positive experience.

Provide design direction.
An important benefit of early user studies is that they can help to provide a direction for system design when none is known. They also help when conflicts arise within the development team, particularly in early phases when features are being identified and implementation discussed. Presenting design alternatives to users at critical early stages can help to resolve these conflicts. User preferences should guide system development.

Encourage user involvement.
When users are brought into the process at the beginning, they perceive that they are important contributors to the development. This encourages them to become involved in other stages of the design, particularly the user testing phase, when their participation is critical. In addition, it helps users to support product development in general, and positively affects their attitude to the new product.

The advantages of early user studies are varied and will depend on the work that has already been invested, as well as the time and resources available. A single study might not provide all the advantages; sometimes it requires more than one study to get successful results. Project needs must be identified and studies designed to achieve that goal. However, any early user study can help in product development. Even those early studies that only serve to verify the current approach to the design are valuable in checking whether the design is headed in the right direction. Such verification (or refusal) of the design approach can save time and resources if the direction changes or problems arise later in development.

How to Select, Design, and Perform Early User Studies

Choosing the type of study and designing it appropriately is a skill that is developed over time. With a variety of experiences, a number of factors come into play that can help direct study design by determining what studies to perform, how many subjects to involve, and how much time to spend on studies.

Evaluate the nature of the task

Consider the goals of the project and what users will be doing to accomplish those goals. If the task will require the user to be mobile, then the system must support a portable solution. You might observe users in their mobile state to determine, for instance, what additional factors come into play when they use the system. If the system will require extensive preliminary training before use, then users' goals for training must be identified, and system functionality designed to support it. Interviews might be appropriate for gathering data about users' goals for training. The environment where the product will be used, the presence of other users, and the relationship of this system to other processes already in place must be considered in understanding the tasks that users must accomplish. These factors will help to indicate what studies make the most sense for the system under development.

Evaluate the state of the technology

Look at what users are currently doing to accomplish the task the new system will address. If an on-line system is already in place, it might be appropriate to test the existing software to understand what users like and dislike about it. User interviews might be important as well, particularly if the system has been in place for some time and users have strong opinions about its functionality. Even if there is no system in place and the one under development introduces users to completely new functionality, studies might be conducted to see how to integrate it smoothly into its target environment. Such studies could involve looking at other tasks the targeted user group currently undertakes and how the technology might change it. Another possibility is to observe an alternative group of users who perform tasks similar to those the new technology will introduce. Other studies might include some competitive benchmarking of other products that perform similar tasks to the new system.

Spend enough time, include enough users

Once studies are designed, be sure to dedicate enough time and users to generate a sufficient range of possible responses. While there is no precise formula to determine how much time or how many users are enough, here are some tips to follow:

Include at least five users, ten or more if possible.

Even when time is short, try to allow enough to observe, interview, or test at least five users. Fewer than five probably will not be able to weed out the users who are anomalies, or whose behavior or opinion is tainted. Five users, while obviously not enough for a statistical majority, can indicate clear opinions that will help determine results. The more users included the better, although the desired number is not infinite because of obvious time and budget constraints. Ten users are often adequate for obtaining useful results, especially in the early stages. However, more or fewer might be appropriate—the time needed or the availability of users might dictate the actual number of subjects who can reasonably be studied.

Get a balance of unbiased user types.

Once the number of users to study is determined, identify who the subjects will be. The most important factor in determining this is to find people as close as possible in character to the target users of the system. Sometimes writing a profile of the target user helps to determine appropriate subjects. Do not include users who are too close to the development process, or who might be tainted by what they already know. The engineers building the system are not appropriate subjects for most user studies (although they might be in special cases where they match the profile of the typical user).Consider other factors such as: Does the study reveal confidential information? Do subjects need to be internal to the company developing the system? You might want subjects to sign a confidentiality agreement before participating.

Try to involve a balance of subjects to cover the range of target users. User age, gender, experience, or nationality might play a role in gathering such a range of users. (For more information, see Chapter 7, Usability Testing.)

Keep individual user sessions limited in time.

Spend enough time with users to allow them to express themselves. In user-observation sessions, you might spend hours or even days watching subjects perform their tasks. Consider the task and how often the types of behavior you are looking for occur. Where you only observe, without interrupting their work, you might need extended periods of time to get results. However, in one-on-one situations you might ask the subject to dedicate an hour to an hour-and-a-half to discussing a current process or the potential of a new system. More than that often results in fidgety subjects who become distracted from the interviewer or the test. Even people who are thrilled to be subjects often fade after about an hour-and-a-half.

Look for patterns in user behavior or responses.

When more than one subject starts to do or say the same thing, chances are you've discovered something important about the task or system. These patterns will help identify desired functions, or provide information about the way a feature should be presented to users. Similarly, differences in behavior or responses probably indicate that the feature is not really important, or might be approached from a different angle.

If results are ambiguous, keep going.

If the subjects do not reveal patterns, then you might need to bring in more subjects to determine whether the subject pool was unbalanced, or if the study's tasks or goals are indecisive or inadequate. Additional subjects will probably be useful if you started with the minimum of five subjects noted previously.

You'll know it when you see it.

Some user studies can lead to inconclusive results. More often, however, they reveal solid findings that will help to direct the design process. These findings can present themselves after studying two or three subjects, and then the rest of the subjects serve primarily as additional support. If genius is the perception of the obvious, then the greatest thing about many early user studies is that the results are so obvious, you cannot believe you didn't know them before the study was conducted.

Record the user study

An important part of a user study is recording the information gathered. While it is critical to gather information first-hand, either by conducting the study or by observing it, it is equally important to make a record for later referral. Taking notes during the study is one way to record the results, but it should not be the only method. Note taking is an excellent way to capture your thoughts, but it can interfere with the flow of interaction between you and the participants. While you concentrate on expressing your thoughts in writing, you might miss an important event of the study. During interviews, copious note taking can be distracting or discomfiting to the subject.

Other recording methods let you note everything without distracting from the study itself. Videotaping is an excellent way to record the session. If that is not possible—either because of availability or objection by participants—audio taping is a viable alternative. You will still probably want to take some notes during the study, but you will not have to worry about recording the details because you can get them by reviewing the tape.

You should obtain permission from your subjects to record the session. Some subjects will object initially, but when you explain that the tapes are for documentation purposes only, most agree to the taping. You will need to devote additional time to reviewing the tapes; however, the results will be well worth the effort.

Another excellent reason to perform video recording is that you then have an unarguable account of what transpired; you can convince others (peers, team members, management) of the validity of your findings. If all you have are notes from your studies, then you might get into a "my word against yours" situation. If you have tape to back you up, there is no arguing about what really happened.

Method 1:User Observation

The study of people performing an activity in their normal work setting or natural environment.

One of the most effective ways to conduct early research is to simply observe users: watch what they do and how they do it, note their setting, their interactions with each other, their use of materials, and the results they achieve.

It is critical to watch users without interrupting them to ask questions or to explain a task. User observation can be conducted in conjunction with other research, but the other research should be kept separate from user observation, if possible. Other methods, such as interviewing, can follow after the findings from the observation are determined.

Figure 3.1 User observation video clip. This user observation for a study of the way people use multimedia tools shows a picture of a designer in his studio framed by much of his development equipment. An important part of user observation is to capture the user the way he currently works - to see the environment, the setup and the components of his tasks.

The importance of user observation

Successful user observations will:

Describe the state of the environment.

You will gather information about the setting and factors that are used (or ignored) by people in accomplishing tasks. This can help to determine characteristics of the system you are building, as well as reveal relationships that might be critical to the user in carrying out tasks.

Find out what users like and don't like.
Users are excellent critics of the existing systems, whether they are technology-dependent or not. By observing current situations, you can identify desired function and interaction for a future system.

Help you to see what works and what doesn't.
Opinions alone are not the only measure of a system's success. By observing users at work, you can see what they like, and what does or does not work. This also can help to shape function and interaction.

Uncover real-world metaphors that might work in your system.
Watching the existing system can help you to identify parallels that you can carry over to the new system. Seeing the users' actions and environment can generate new ideas for visually and semantically organizing on-line tasks in the new design.

Steps for observing users

1. Identify the profile of a "typical" user (or users).

2. Decide how many users to include in the study.

3. Contact users who fit this profile.

4. Request permission to observe.

5. Prepare to document the observation with audio, video, or multiple observation teams.

6. Watch users in action to analyze the current situation.

7. Make note of user actions and any design ideas that come to you during the observation.

Hints/suggestions

Remember:

- Observe without interruption.

- Observe enough users to get valid data.

Implement this study method:

- Before design begins to generate ideas.

- During the development cycle to evaluate development concepts.

- At the end of the development cycle to analyze the product's functionality.

Exercise task

Plan and conduct a user observation for your supermarket guide. Select a supermarket appropriate for your observation, visit that market, and observe users (remember to ask permission first).

Before you conduct the studies, you must decide the following:

- How much time will you spend in a single observation session?

- How many observation sessions do you want to conduct?

- How will you record the sessions?

When you conduct the studies, you will probably want to address the following questions:

- What kind of information do people want?

- What kind of information is already available to them?

- How do they use it?

- Where do people go now to get information in the super-market?

- What kinds of features will be appropriate in your guide?

- Are there any concepts in use that you might model in the new system?

Method 2: User Interviews

One-on-one sessions with potential users to discuss the methods currently in place and/or their expectations or requirements for a future system.

Talking to users about their current system and about their ideas and hopes for a future system can provide valuable information about what they really want their software to do. The best way to gather information from users is to put together a list of questions or topics based on the goals of the system. This list can serve as a general format for an interview. Conduct a number of such interviews with different potential users.

The length of a single interview session will depend on how much information you plan to gather from each participant. In general, you will want to spend between 45 and 90 minutes with each subject. Less time than that will often not give the users time to really open up and share their thoughts. More time than that might make the subjects uneasy or cause them to give quick, shallow responses in the hope of ending the session soon. Keep subjects at ease and focused on the content of the interview.

Conduct the interview in a comfortable, informal, and natural setting. For example, use their offices when you are interviewing about work practices, or their living rooms if you are exploring ideas for a home entertainment system. Being in their own environment puts them at ease, and lets them point out how they approach a task, or factors that are important to them about their setting.

Interviews are usually conducted in conjunction with other types of user studies. After a user observation is complete, you might enlist some of the subjects from the observation as interview subjects. This is particularly helpful in situations where you want to clarify behavior that occurred in the observation, or inquire about their goals for tasks you observed. It is important in these cases to conduct interviews after the observations are complete, so as not to taint the observation outcome.

Interviews can take a variety of formats. You can ask questions and take notes, have the subject complete a questionnaire, or a combination of these approaches. Typically, more informal interviews follow a formal question-answer session. For more formal results, scaled-response questionnaires (such as when 1 represents "I strongly agree" and 5 represents "I strongly disagree") will help to generate sound, statistically valid responses. A discussion format might also be appropriate—you present general topics and ask the subject to comment on them. The format of the interview should derive from the nature of the information being gathered. Listen carefully to the subjects' concerns and be careful not to direct their answers by providing too much information.

The importance of user interviews

Like user observations, user interviews reveal valuable information about the goals of users. We can discover what users really think about system features or components. Users often have excellent ideas about how to improve the existing system. Users can provide a wealth of knowledge—all we have to do is ask them!

```
  ○   Printer User Interview

      Name:_____
      Date:_____

      1.  Did the printer perform adequately?  Why (not)?

      2.  Describe your communication with the
          printer/computer.  How did you interface
          with each?  Did you ever have to go back and
          forth (multiple times) to achieve desired
          results?  Were there any parts of the interface
          you wish had been on the other machine?

      3.  Any functions the printer didn't
          (couldn't) perform?

  ○   4.  Was there ever a time when feedback was
          inadequate?  Any time when you might have liked
          instruction for some task?

      5.  What can you tell me about the lights on the
          printer?  How many are there?  Did you notice
          how they behave (on, off, blinking, color)?

      6.  Did you use the manual feed?  How was the
          interface there?

      7.  Have you ever set up a printer?  What was the
          process you used?  Any comments?

      8.  Have you ever needed help when printing?  What
          did you do?

  ○   9.  Anything else about the printer or observation
          you would like to comment on?
```

Figure 3.2 Sample text from user interviews. User interviews help you to assess users opinions and responses to your studies. You formulate the questions or discussion points for the interview based on your goals for the software—they should address such issues as what are you trying to learn about the software, what functions are you trying to evaluate, what points do you think are critical to users? This segment of an interview was used to compliment a user observation of laser printer users.

The advantages of user interviews

Appropriately conducted user interviews will:

Reveal users' thoughts.

Take advantage of interview sessions to obtain not only answers to the questions, but also the users' opinions and thoughts. If the interview takes a different turn from the one you had planned, check to see if the user is trying to tell you something important before steering him or her back to the topic. Users can provide significant information about something you might not have originally planned to discuss.

Make comparisons with other technologies or processes.

Ask users to compare the process or system you are studying with others with which they are familiar. You might have some comparisons in mind that you would like the user to discuss. Ask the user to draw parallels to a similar process. Having users make comparisons can be an excellent way to understand how they think about a task. Users can also offer design suggestions or likely metaphors on which the user interface could be based.

Generate design alternatives.

By having users talk about what they like and don't like about various system features or components, you provide them with an opportunity to make suggestions for alternative designs. Your interview subjects are "experts" at the system or task you are studying. They have probably been thinking about ways to improve an existing system, and what they would omit from a future system.

Steps for interviewing users

1. Identify the profile of "typical" users for your system.

2. Draft the goals of your interview. Identify what you hope to learn.

3. Use these goals to develop questions or discussion points for the interview. Be sure that each of your desired goals is addressed in at least one question.

4. Consider using statistical data gathering methods, if appropriate. Sometimes questionnaires that use a scale to rate answers (such as the 1-10 Likert scale) allows users to express themselves more candidly than a direct response to your verbal questions.

5. Determine how many interviews you will conduct.

6. Contact users who fit your profile and schedule a time for each interview.

7. Prepare to document the interview with audio, video, or an additional observer.

8. Conduct the interviews.

9. Note responses to the questions and topics, as well as any other points of interest that arise.

Hints/suggestions

• Plan adequate time between interviews to allow for sessions that run over, or simply for you to take a break.

• Spread the interviews over a period of time; conducting too many in one day can be exhausting. For instance, if you are planning a dozen interviews, you might want to schedule four a day for three days.

• As with other early user studies, conduct interviews before design has begun, if possible.

• Link interviews with user observations, interviewing users after observing them.

• Plan your interviews to make the best use of your subjects' time.

- Try not to ask leading questions that supply the user with potential answers.

- Encourage the user to give independent responses.

Exercise task

Design and conduct user interviews for your supermarket guide. Decide whether you will interview users at the supermarket, or at some other time and place. You might want to interview users from more than one supermarket. Develop interview questions that will guide you in building your interactive system. Your goals for your sessions will probably be similar to those for your user observation, and will include answers to questions such as:

- What do people want to know as they shop at the supermarket?

- What kind of information is already available and how is it used?

- Where do people go now to get information in the supermarket?

- How much time do users think they would spend with such a guide?

- Where do users want the guide to be located (in a standing central location, on grocery carts, at food displays)?

Method 3: Task Analysis

An in-depth study of a task and how it is performed.

Sometimes it is useful to look closely at how users accomplish a task. Task analysis is a special case of user observation that focuses on the process users follow, rather than on general concerns such as their likes and dislikes. Understanding each component of the whole process can help to show which parts will lend themselves to the new system. Task analysis of the process often takes little time. It can be an excellent early user study to help with the design of a system.

Task analysis is particularly valuable when the process being replaced is non-technical. For example, suppose a new on-line system is being developed to replace a process that is currently accomplished using paper forms. Even though the current and the new processes might not seem to have much in common, you can gather an enormous amount of information by observing how the current task is done. Some of the steps accomplished with paper will need to be translated to an on-line form. At the same time, parts of the process that can be automated or improved through an on-line system will become evident when analyzing the limitations of the current process.

Task analysis can be equally valuable when the system being developed is an evolution of a technology in place. This is especially true when the system in place isn't working well. Conducting a task analysis can help developers step back from what is known about specific user problems, design issues, and flaws. When a lot of time has been devoted to a project, developers sometimes make assumptions they do not question. Those assumptions can be misleading about what is actually going on with the users of the system. A correctly-conducted task analysis leaves no room for false assumptions. This list of tasks must then be reviewed to understand what is really going on in order to plan a future iteration of a design.

Task analysis is rarely the only type of user study conducted as pre-design research. It is usually conducted in combination with interviews or more general user observations. While a task analysis can be useful, it is probably more revealing when the results of the analysis are used to generate questions and discussion points for later interviews. Conducting interviews after a task analysis allows you to make hypotheses about what is working and suggest improvements. You should then check out these hypotheses and suggestions with the system's users.

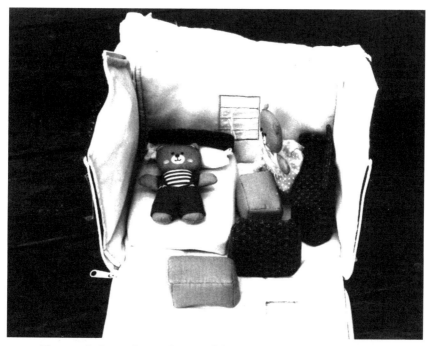

Figure 3.3 Task analysis of furniture manipulation. This child's toy exemplifies that high technology solutions are not needed to analyze what users do in their current approach to something. A doll house such as this can be used to help users explain how they think about moving furniture around in their own living rooms. Having physical representations of the furniture, even in the form of toys, is extremely useful for helping describe the manipulations they might make or the orientation of the furniture as it is moved.

The importance of task analysis

Task analysis is an excellent way to evaluate the current process objectively. Since it is a study of the precise steps that make up a process, results are not tempered by the personal opinions of the users or the researchers.

The advantages of task analysis

Some of the benefits of task analysis are that it allows you to:

Develop a detailed description of the task your technology addresses.

Simply observing users to understand what they do and why they do it is important for several reasons. When you are building a system that will introduce technology to a currently low-tech function, understanding the current steps and incorporating them (when appropriate) in the new design can ease the transition for users. When you have problems with an existing system and are not sure why, task analysis can point out issues you might have overlooked.

Evaluate the user interface currently in place.

All products and processes present a user interface through which people interact, whether or not it's a computer-based system. Performing a task analysis can help to identify what information is given to users, how they enter information into the system, and where they make choices for interaction. This can help point out elements important in the user interface you are developing for your system.

Reveal users' knowledge of a task.

Task analysis reveals the ability users have to perform a task. It identifies the tools currently used to perform the task, and points out how users apply these tools. It might show that users apply tools in similar or in diverse ways. Likewise, task analysis can indicate the constraints and limitations of the current system.

Map the task from the users' point of view.

Even though you are not directly asking users to express their point of view during a task analysis, you gather information about their approach by watching. This can reveal interesting data, particularly if you conduct task analysis with multiple users and then compare the results.

Identify critical design elements.

Examining each step the user takes in a process can often present exciting design ideas. Seeing the progression of events and identifying the tools currently in place can provide ideas for functionality or appearance in the new system.

Steps for conducting a task analysis

1. Identify the task that you will evaluate.

2. Find someone (or some people) who regularly performs the task you are studying.

3. Watch the person (people) perform the task.

4. Record the steps of the task, in order, using video if possible.

5. Note the knowledge this person has at each step, and any problems encountered.

6. Interview the person who performs the task.

7. Review your notes to create a table or map of the task.

Hints/suggestions

• During the observation, try not to read too much into why users do what they do. The purpose is to understand objectively what they do. Analyzing the why comes later.

• Conduct a task analysis at the beginning of a project, before design begins.

• Conduct a task analysis together with a user observation or as an earlier step to a user interview.

• Don't assume you already know what people will do. At the very least, a task analysis will help you verify your approach; more often than not, it will also present new information that can be critical to your design.

Exercise task

Plan and conduct a task analysis of people gathering information in a supermarket. You might do this in conjunction with your general user observation, or conduct it as a separate study. Identify a location in the supermarket where people go to get information (such as the manager's office or a checkout stand) and wait there until people come to get information. Or follow a clerk around and wait for people to approach with questions. In either case, take note of everything that happens when supermarket shoppers try to get information. You'll want to address these questions:

- How did they know where to come to get information?

- What kinds of questions do they ask?

- What kinds of responses do they get?

- Are the people happy with the responses, or do they probe further?

- Do people typically ask one or more than one question?

- Do people record the responses in any way?

- If the information desired is not available, what do people do?

Method 4: Expert Interviews

One-on-one or group sessions with people who know a great deal about the users of the system, or who are highly experienced with the technology.

Like user interviews, expert interviews allow you to obtain first-hand information from people with valuable opinions. Unlike user interviews, however, experts will seldom give you direct feedback on the system under development. Instead, they provide indirect ways to explore user behavior or requirements. Expert interviews are most useful as ways to research the technology in place, or the technology needed to support the system you are building. Think of expert interviews as background research that allows you to get information—not from the people who will use your system, but from people who have some unique and informative perspective about the system's users.

Typically, you will conduct only a few expert interviews, for two reasons. One, because there will not be many experts available to interview. Two, it doesn't require numerous expert interviews to gather the information you seek. You will not need to interview as many experts as you will users. With user interviews, you are polling a number of users to see if there is consensus on important development issues, after weeding out individual biases. With expert interviews, gathering a large amount of expert data from ten or more experts and analyzing it for significance is a waste of time and energy. However, each system and technology is unique. The number of expert interviews you require will depend on the nature of your task and the resources available to you.

Conduct expert interviews before design on the project truly begins. Since expert interviews are research for your technology and can provide a wealth of information, it might be strategic to conduct them before any other early user studies. The information you obtain about the users and their environments will be valuable in shaping the goals and contents of user observations or user interviews.

Expert interviews can also be helpful after other early studies are completed. Experts can help you analyze the data, point out behavior patterns, or detect user motivation. These interviews are typically informal. Prepare some questions. Present your findings and describe your impressions. Ask for a verification or opinion. Experts might be just the design partners you need to help understand the complexities of user behavior or the requirements for your developing system.

Figure 3.4 Video of an expert interview. Paul Zimmerman, the architect shown in this figure, was interviewed as an expert for a project to design 3D interaction methods. He talked about his experiences in interpreting what his clients wanted in 3D space, his methods of designing new spaces and communicating his designs to his clients. His approach set a foundation for later interactive prototypes and 3D manipulation tools.

The importance of expert interviews

Experts offer a critical perspective to your system design, one other user studies cannot capture. Expert interviews should be conducted in conjunction with other user studies.

Advantages of expert interview

Some of the advantages of expert interviews are that they:

Allow you to find out about users when you can't talk to them directly.

While there is no substitute for direct user contact, there are times when users are unavailable as study subjects. Experts who regularly deal with the users of your system will be able to tell you about them. Even when users are around, there might be times when your interaction is limited due to time, distance, expense, or resource constraints.

Help you design subsequent user studies.

Expert interviews can help you design and conduct efficient, useful studies with your users.

Help you see the system from another point of view.

It is often true that experts have been in contact with your technology or users far longer than you have. As a result, they have developed theories on user motivation and goals that will help you decide on a direction to pursue or to round out your design plans.

Help to research a technology.

Rather than providing information about users, some experts will be able to provide information on the workings of your technology or system. Their insights might prove valuable when designing the interface. The experts also might have materials useful for developing prototypes or for making presentations to your users and others to help them understand the system.

Offer design ideas.

At the very least, experts offer alternative opinions and points of view on the system you are developing. Since they have been around the technology and the users for a long time, they probably have ideas about how to improve the technology or make users' task easier. These ideas can help you in the early phases of design and later as you refine the design.

Steps for interviewing experts

1. Identify your experts, drawing on people with significant knowledge about your technology, your target users, or both.

2. Identify your goals for the interview and what you hope to learn.

3. Develop questions or discussion points for the interview, making sure each goal is addressed with at least one question. You might vary your interview format depending on the subject of the interviews.

4. Contact your subjects and schedule the interviews.

5. Prepare to document the interview with audio, video, or an additional observer.

6. Conduct the interviews.

7. Use any information gathered to help direct further user studies.

Hints/suggestions

- Take advantage of any experts available to you. Don't worry about trying to eliminate bias in the case of experts.

- Think of these interviews as research.

- Keep the interviews informal and friendly.

- Touch base with your experts later to check your findings or get additional feedback.

- Not all experts will be directly linked to the technology or process—sometimes they can come from unconventional connections.

Exercise task

Plan and conduct expert interviews for the supermarket guide. Consider the resources available to you at the supermarket and at other locations. Some "experts" you might think about are:

- Grocers, check-out clerks, and delivery people at the supermarket.

- Supermarket managers, and others responsible for organizing food displays and other information management tasks.

- People you know who are super supermarket users—those who do a lot of shopping.

- People who put together supermarket flyers for local newspapers or mail delivery.

- Someone who has actually designed an electronic supermarket information system, or some other electronic guide with a similar function.

Method 5: Seed Studies

Studies of a process over time, where the person being studied keeps track of conditions and activities at designated intervals.

Some user studies require a significant amount of time. The process being studied might happen over many days, or the user interaction might be interspersed with numerous other activities. Since it is impractical to follow a user for days, a seed study could be the solution. You seed the users with the information and tools necessary to record results and note observations, so that they are active participants in the study.

A seed study requires users to record information at either regular or irregular time intervals. Users might enter the same information each time, or the information gathered might depend on the circumstances. Make the participant's task as simple and straightforward as possible. Provide a simple way for subjects to record the data; and, if you don't want users to tire quickly of gathering the data, make each information-gathering occasion as brief as possible.

Figure 3.5 Seed study recording device. This hand-held tape recorder was used in a seed study to follow a person's daily activities with home appliances. The questions taped to the front of the recorder reminded users what to say each time they recorded some information. The small device could easily be carried around and used by participants.

Like other early user studies, seed studies can help to identify the critical elements of the users' processes. The difference is that a seed study requires active participation from the user. Since the user is consciously contributing information, there is a risk that the information gathered is not as objective as in other studies. Don't tell them too much about why you want the information they are gathering. If participants do not know very much about the goals of the study, they will be more objective during the information-gathering phase. However, you will have to tell users something about the study to help interest them in participating and to motivate them during the information-gathering phase. Use statements that lead to direct and honest information without influencing the user. For example, "We are looking to see if you complete these tasks in approximately the same amount of time." Or, "We are gathering data about how what you do differs from what other people do."

In seed studies, information is recorded at different times and under different conditions so you can understand the types of tasks that happen over extended periods of time. Since seed studies actively engage participants in data gathering, they offer insight into the different approaches taken by different subjects. While different subjects' approaches might also be determined from other studies conducted by impartial users, seed studies ensure that the data is untainted by the opinions of the person conducting the study.

The importance of seed studies

Seed studies provide a way to gather information that would otherwise be unobtainable with more traditional observation and study methods. They give you a way to gather information over extended periods of time, allowing users to participate with minimal interference to their normal routines.

Advantages of seed studies

The advantages of seed studies are that they:

Qualify the user's point of view of a task or process.

Since the users themselves are active participants in gathering information, the data expresses their points of view about what they are doing. If understanding the subjects' point of view is important to your study, be sure to ask the users to provide information that addresses their thoughts or intent at the time of data entry.

Identify if activities are dependent on certain factors.

Ask users to record precisely what they are doing at the information-gathering intervals. That way you learn whether what they are doing depends on other activities or factors. If this is particularly important to your study, have users make note of any dependencies.

Help you understand the interrelation of the various elements in a process.

Processes that occur over time often involve multiple elements and depend on the interrelation of those elements. Understanding these relationships might be critical in the design of your new system. Give users a question to respond to that addresses the interrelation of process elements.

Generate ideas for design.

As with other early user studies, seed studies can be important and innovative ways to generate design ideas for your new system. Design ideas will seem especially suitable when they are provided by multiple subjects, or when the same design idea occurs on multiple occasions to the same person.

Show how people really use the technology.

Seed studies might be the only way to get a handle on how people use a technology over long periods of time. They enable you to observe what different people are doing with that technology over time. It might be the most realistic way of evaluating a process.

Steps for conducting a seed study

1. Find one or more people who regularly perform the activity you want to study.

2. Identify the information you want them to record.

3. Decide on the appropriate method for recording the activity. The subjects might carry around a portable audio tape recorder and speak into it, or a pen and pad of paper for writing responses.

4. Determine the time intervals when the subjects will record the information: regular intervals, (such as every two hours) or more irregular intervals. You might want to equip the subjects with a preprogrammed alarm clock as a reminder to record the information.

5. Send off your subjects to gather the information.

6. Analyze the information, using charts or graphs for comparison.

7. Make recommendations based on your findings.

Hints/suggestions

- As with other studies, conduct seed studies before design begins in order to generate ideas.

- Seed studies can also be excellent ways to evaluate your designs as the technology develops. You might choose to "seed" subjects with a prototype of the system to see how people use your technology over time.

- Sometimes the information-gathering sessions are intrusive to participants, particularly if they happen at random intervals and catch them in the middle of something else. In that case, offer them the opportunity to postpone the data gathering to another more opportune time.

Exercise task

Develop a seed study that is appropriate for learning what kinds of information are important to supermarket shoppers. Because seed studies are best for understanding processes that happen over longer periods of time, and supermarket shoppers typically conduct their shopping activity in an hour or less, this study will probably not that take place in the supermarket. Spend some time imagining what type of process occurs over time while users are away from the supermarket. Consider the following issues:

- How will you engage participants?

- How many subjects will you include?

- What types of information will you gather?

- Will participants answer specific questions, or respond to statements?

- What is the appropriate time interval for recording information? Every morning? Twice a day? Hourly? The interval will probably depend on the type of information you request.

- How will participants record their data? You might want to use preprinted forms that they fill in each time, or an audio-recording device. You might want subjects to call and leave a message with the information on a voice mail system.

- How will you process the data?

Method 6: Evaluating Early Designs

Review and critique of an application or system in its early phases.

In the ideal development world, system builders conduct all necessary research before they begin designing a new application or system. In the real world, research rarely precedes system development. While a preliminary application or system might have been developed before any user studies were made, it has the benefit of existing. If you are lucky, this work was intended as a prototype—in this event, at least, system developers recognize the need for evolution and change. In any case, an existing system should not be overlooked while studies and research are conducted. Instead, evaluate the existing design and use your findings to help direct your studies from this point forward.

Making good use of an existing design can help with the design of your user-oriented system. Use what exists to answer a number of questions that might help you define appropriate studies to conduct or determine design paths to follow. Evaluating an existing design can help you to understand how the developers envision implementing the system. This is important information to have before you make your study findings and recommendations. You will also have a better understanding of your audience so you can work together as an interdisciplinary team.

Something you should know about the existing design is whether users were involved at all before or during its development. Even if user involvement was limited to a friend who met the profile of the target user, the reasoning then applied to system development might be helpful in understanding the design.

A big advantage to an existing design—even if it is only drawings of potential screen designs—is that it can be presented to users for feedback. If an interactive on-line prototype exists, it can be used as part of a more directed user study to see how users respond to the emerging system.

When evaluating an existing design, look for what the design tells you about the developing technology. Often an existing implementation is a better way to understand what the developers had in mind in building the technology than discussions alone. You can begin to see the technology at work, and possibly understand what your potential designs can do, or how they might be constrained by implementation details. Discuss the design with system developers, and find out how flexible they are on various implementation details. Some features of the system are actually constrained by the technology, and it is necessary to understand this at early stages of the design.

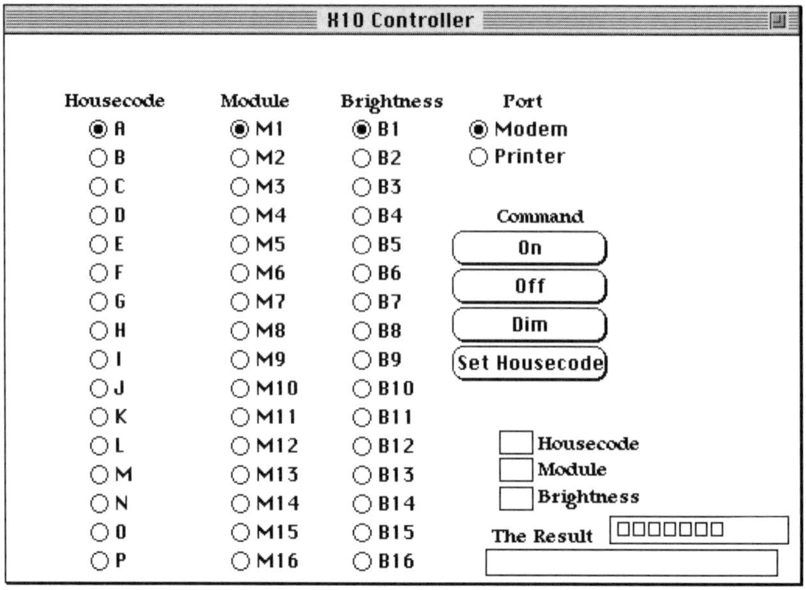

Figure 3.6 Early design for home control system. This HyperCard stack shows the basic application for accessing the appliance control units that make up the X10 System (circa 1989). Radio buttons are used to represent groupings of up to 16 options, with simple text buttons for actions and small type in boxes for presenting numerical information. The screen is cluttered and functionality is unlabeled and unclear. This implementation reflects the underlying structure of the system rather than how users see or apply system functionality. In a project later undertaken to apply a user-centered design approach to this application, the user interface significantly changed to reflect what users wanted in the design and interaction. (See figures 5.2 and 5.3 for evolutions of the design of this Home Control System.)

The importance of evaluating early designs

Evaluation of existing works can have a number of advantages for further system development, especially when the implementation team says further development is necessary. Some of the ways early designs can be used are to:

Take advantage of work that has already been done.

The best reason for using early or existing designs is that they are there. In the worst case, you will end up discarding the entire work, but you might learn both positive and negative things about the system that exists. Don't ignore an existing work just because it wasn't designed with the same goals you have in mind.

Allow you to experience the system as a user.

Since you have an example of the technology in action, you can begin to evaluate the technology by using it yourself. You won't have to guess at how others might use it.

Offer insight into the developers' point of view.

Evaluating the existing system will teach you something about what the developers had in mind for the system implementation. You can use this information to help guide you in your recommendations or later study findings. It is important, however, to remain a distant and objective evaluation—try not to assume that elements of the interface have to be in the ways they currently are presented. While developers are sometimes constrained by the technology, more often than not they are predisposed to certain ideas because of their understanding of the problem. Remain impartial so you can ask for what is best for users.

Generate design ideas.

By evaluating what works and what doesn't about an early design, you will begin to generate alternative ideas for future versions. Design ideas might be for specific solutions in the user interface or for user studies that you might want to conduct. Questions you have about certain implementation details might help direct you to appropriate user studies, or to the issues that those studies should address.

Provide a way to give feedback to developers at early stages.

If you include a written evaluation or a presentation to developers as part of your evaluation process, you provide critical feedback to the design team at early stages of the design. This feedback might help developers to direct their work to best meet user needs.

You might think that existing work limits the possibility of further design. This is true only when the early designs are not looked at objectively, and they are assumed to be the basis of further design because they already exist. If you adopt the attitude that existing designs are helpful for evaluation but that they are not necessarily the final system configuration, you will be able to put your existing designs to work for you.

Steps for conducting an early design evaluation

1. Get the most up-to-date version of the design you will be evaluating.

2. Conduct a preliminary review of the design to understand its basic functions. Get a demonstration from the implementors, if possible, and discuss the design with them.

3. Draft a document that presents your goals for evaluating the design and the criteria you will use to evaluate it.

4. Think about specific tasks or exercises you can follow through the design that will enable you to "test it out" in an appropriate way. Choose tasks for which the system really will be used.

5. Use your goals and your criteria to document specific tasks in evaluating the design. Note your thoughts and reactions as you are using the system.

6. Document your findings and present them to system developers.

7. Use what you know about the existing design to plan additional user studies.

Hints/suggestions

- Try to be impartial in evaluating the design—don't think about how your findings might limit future work.

- Engage colleagues to help you evaluate the design. Additional feedback might help you to make the best use of the existing system.

- Think of yourself as a user in a user test—what do you really want to do with this system, and how is the design helping or impeding that?

- As you evaluate the design, think about both the existing problems and what works well. If something works well, the developers have already solved some of your design challenges.

Exercise task

Try to locate an existing implementation of an on-line supermarket guide, and evaluate it as an early design for your system. You might have to conduct some research to find such a guide, since they are obviously not available at every neighborhood supermarket. Newspapers and magazines in recent years have reviewed such systems, and local supermarket employees who are technology buffs might be able to help you. If you are lucky enough to find one, some of the questions to address during your evaluation are:

- What does this system do?

- What functions does it provide to the user?

- What doesn't this system do?

- Who are the target users for this system? Think about demographics, frequency of shopping activity, and time necessary to spend with the system.

- Where is this system used?

- What are the positive and negative points of this system?

- What is the technology involved in presenting this system and how effective is it?

- Can I talk to the person/people who designed and built this system?

If you cannot find an on-line implementation, you might evaluate a related on-line information guide, such as a guide at a mall ar department store. You will not be able to obtain information specifically relating to supermarket guides, but you will still gather useful information for designing on-line guides in general.

Chapter 4

Off-line Tools and Procedures

What Are Off-line Tools and Procedures?

Many kinds of computer software can be designed without going anywhere near a computer. Because they are not on-line computer prototypes, I refer to them as off-line designs—they can be built using off-line tools and procedures. These tools and procedures include writing a description of the way a new system will work, making paper and pencil drawings, or constructing models using a variety of other conventional materials: scissors, matte knife, white glue, and so forth.

Almost all designers I know are capable of writing a description of a system, or at least describing it to someone else who can write it for them. Art materials, such as different weight and textured drawing surfaces, marking tools in a variety of colors and textures, and other materials such as cardboard, foam core board, masonite, wooden plyboard, Plexiglas, Styrofoam, telephone cabling and other hardware, can all be valuable for building prototypes of

65

your application or system design. I encourage you to experiment with different media and find what you like best for communicating your designs. Your local art store is the best place to start looking for innovative ways to express the specifics of your design.

Creative combinations of materials can lead to effective models that represent parts of your system. You can use these off-line designs in user studies to obtain feedback on the progress of the design, or to gather further design ideas. Off-line designs might be stories read to potential users to see if they agree with your plans for the developing technology. They might be drawings of potential computer screens, or even less committal sketches of the way a technology could be used in the new system. Off-line designs can be more complex models used to simulate parts of the user interface, such as scrolling windows, or the layout of fields on the screen, or interactive events that occur in response to some user action. Combining storytelling with drawings or models can help piece together the elements of a design that can then be further developed by the members of a design team.

Off-line tools can be used at various phases of a design, but they are particularly useful in the early stages, when concepts are beginning to form but no commitment to a specific implementation has been made. Off-line tools and procedures often follow early user studies, and can quickly and inexpensively develop some of the ideas that have come out of these studies. Off-line tools and procedures are also important as the design evolves, to test ideas and see what makes sense for implementation. Whether these designs are shown to potential users for feedback, or to other members of the design team during development phases, or are simply built by an individual to validate an idea, off-line designs can be extremely valuable to a user interface designer.

Almost everyone I know has had experience with the kinds of off-line tools and procedures that I advocate. While some of the techniques are taught in more advanced art or design programs, the basic processes are easily adapted to things we already know how to use. Some of us might not have used these procedures since grade school, but these are not tools we forget how to use or that are difficult to relearn. Off-line tools encourage you to use the creative elements that come most naturally to you—be they storytelling, drawing, building, or tinkering. Creating off-line designs can be extremely rewarding because the results are quickly visible and tactile. And best of all, creating off-line designs is usually fun, because it gives you a chance to get down and dirty with the design that you have been researching and thinking about.

The Advantages of Off-line Tools and Procedures

Off-line tools and procedures are valuable in user interface development for many reasons. Some of them are:

Materials are accessible and (usually) cheap.

You can find basic writing and drawing supplies in the stockrooms of even the smallest offices. If you have to buy new supplies, paper and pens are relatively inexpensive, particularly when compared to computer equipment and software. As you gain more experience with the available tools, you will be able to better define the materials that you need. Special purchases will be fairly inexpensive, and you can reuse supplies for later off-line designs. Some advanced designs might require more expense, but you can weigh the cost value trade-off for your specific design. None of the tools or processes in the following sections are inherently costly; and if you are creative in gathering materials, you can usually keep costs low.

Materials and designs are portable.

Most off-line designs can be created in pieces that you can take along to wherever you happen to be working. Unlike on-line design tools, you are not chained to the computer system on your desk. This can be useful during the design process and once designs are ready for demonstration or testing purposes.

They can be worked on by more than one designer simultaneously.

Along with portability comes ease of transfer from one designer to another. If you are working on a design with a colleague, you can each work on separate parts and then combine them, or if it is the type of design that only one person can work on at a time, you can pass it back and forth.

Designs convey more than words.

Actually building the designs instead of simply telling others about them helps you to visualize your ideas and communicate your concept more effectively than words alone can do. Even written descriptions are better than verbal ones. Writing it out helps you to resolve ambiguities or inconsistencies and forces you to think about issues you might not otherwise have addressed. A physical representation (written or constructed) of your design is useful for sharing the concept with fellow designers, system builders (even if this builder is you!), and to potential users.

Training is rarely necessary.

Writing, drawing, and constructing are skills almost everyone has. I'm not talking about writing like Hemingway, drawing like Leonardo da Vinci, or building like Frank Lloyd Wright. Using off-line tools and procedures is not about making beautiful art, but about communicating ideas for the purpose of better design. If you are uncomfortable with your level of skill with drawing or writing, a workshop or seminar might be helpful.

Designs are dispensable.

These designs are fairly dispensable because they are inexpensive and can be built with minimal time or effort. If what you write, draw, or build isn't exactly what's needed, it's fairly simple to write, draw, or build something that is. Typically, you will learn enough about what worked and didn't work after building the first version to ensure that later versions are more successful.

Designs are accessible to all.

Since designs are a combination of basic skills, different designers can contribute to designs in ways that utilize their individual strengths and that build on each other. One designer can add or change another designer's written description of a project. Drawings can be modified easily to communicate a variation on a design concept.While it is true that different members of a design team will have different skill levels, when it comes to writing or drawing, most will have the basic skills necessary to get the point across.

Designs are less committal.

Since the off-line design is not the finished product, it is more likely to elicit constructive criticism and is adaptable to change. Design team members tend to give honest feedback throughout development with off-line designs, because they know that they are not criticizing an end product; they know you will have to build the real system anyway. Additionally, subjects of user studies might be more inclined to tell you how they feel about your design concepts, since they know that what you are showing them is only a transitional step in the design, not the real thing.

They help to clarify designs and lead to other possibilities.

Since most of us can get our ideas across with a pencil fairly easily and quickly, off-line designs require little investment in learning how to make the tools work. As a result, you can spend your time concentrating on the details of the design. This allows you to clarify the design and lead it through necessary changes to build the best design possible before committing to a software architecture or building a time-consuming, working prototype. Remember, off-line designs are not about pretty drawings, but expressions of the design.

Physical designs can be studied and tested.

Off-line designs that model interactivity—either through storyboards, flip-books, or some other mockup technique—offer the added advantage of letting you evaluate or test the interaction. Testing can be done at early stages, before an investment is made (in time or money) in a more complex software design. Obtaining feedback in these early stages allows you to get the basic design right, so that you need to worry about only the less critical details in an on-line version. On-line, you can concentrate on the elements of the design specific to the software that could not be tested on paper.

The possibilities are endless.

The possibilities are endless for the techniques to use and how to use them to create off-line designs. Any creative techniques you can think of can probably be applied to help communicate design ideas. Different applications or systems will lend themselves to various alternatives—adapt your own creative approaches to this process. I have seen these unconventional methods applied successfully to the user interface design process: using unconventional materials, involving people to role-play parts of the system, and creating live theatrical productions that demonstrate the system.

How to Select, Design, and Perform Off-line Tools and Procedures

The array of tool and procedure choices might seem overwhelming, because so many possibilities exist for creating and applying off-line designs to the user interface development process. You will probably not have the time or the need to apply all—or even most of—the off-line techniques for each development project. While there is no one right way to approach any design problem, there are disciplined ways to determine which off-line tools are appropriate for your given design. These are some of the ways to evaluate the tools and procedures:

Determine how much time you have.

You have to evaluate the amount of time you will devote to the entire project, as well as how much of that time will be spent on designing, testing, building, and iterating. It is valuable to establish time estimates for individual prototypes, as well, and to include time for presenting the design to other members of the development team and end users (if appropriate). The actual time spent might differ from your scheduled time. One good way to evaluate time requirements is to work backward from a known due date. Time for each component of the process will depend on the nature of your problem; in general, you will probably want to spend roughly a third of your time on prebuilding studies and designs; a third of your time building the system, and a third of your time testing and rebuilding the system.

Some design problems might require more time up front in preliminary design stages, others might be new implementation technologies that require more programming and/or debugging time. It is important, however, that you spend at least some time devoted to preliminary design. If you dive in and start coding right away, you will find yourself spending large amounts of time later reworking your code to address the needs of an evolving design. It is much better to plan for adequate design time so that during the implementation phase all you really have to worry about is getting the on-line design to work as expected.

See what materials, skills, and resources are available.

One realistic way to evaluate which off-line tools or procedures are appropriate for you is to take inventory of what you have on hand, and evaluate the skills of the people on the design team. If you have an industrial designer on the team and have easy access to building materials, then creating a mockup of your system might be appropriate. If you have a graphic artist on the team, then you might want to concentrate on storyboards of the design. If you don't have either of these professionals on your design team, all is not lost. At the very least, you can write scenarios describing the system design, or do some basic drawing to get visual ideas across. You can hire someone on a contract basis to help with the design stages, or even take a basic course in drawing skills. Remember, off-line designs do not need to be created by professionals. Elementary drawings and mockups can be as valuable as professionally-created design pieces—perhaps even more so, since they are created by the members of the design team who understand the nature of the design problem and are using off-line designs as a way to communicate.

Evaluate what you are going to do with your designs.

Knowing what you will do with your designs will help you determine the procedures to follow. Think about who you are building the designs for. Will you show them to other members of the design team? Hardware engineers who might be responsible for building an actual product? Software implementers responsible for building the designs? Potential end users who will help you to evaluate them as part of a user study? If you are going to visualize a new design for both a hardware and a software product, a physical mockup illustrating your ideas would be appropriate. If you are completing a quick concept-sketch to get ideas across to other members of the design team, drawings or storyboards will do.

Think about how durable designs must be.

Knowing how long you want designs to be around or how much exposure they must undergo might also help you decide what types of designs to develop. If the designs are simply intermediate expressions of ideas and won't leave your office, then you need not worry about the durability of the materials you use. On the other hand, if you plan to use a design for user studies, or to travel on the "demo circuit," then build them to last. Plan to invest more time in the designs that will be around for longer periods of time.

Understand how much you can accomplish off-line.

Off-line designs are an excellent way to express basic user interface elements and interaction and for visualizing designs. However, they are not suitable for testing the specifics of visual details or interactions. You need to move the designs to their target platforms to evaluate whether or not users can discriminate forms or obtain adequate feedback on interactive functions. By knowing what off-line designs are good for, and moving on to other design techniques to accomplish other tasks, you can make the most of your design time.

Work with others.

Off-line techniques provide an excellent opportunity to make good use of multiple members of a design team—to save time in the long run and contribute to a more robust design. Individual team members can work simultaneously on separate designs, each generating storyboards to illustrate a scenario. Then, the team can get together and choose the elements from each of the storyboards that the group thinks best represent the goal. Team members might also work simultaneously on the same design, completing different segments of a scenario or pages in a flipbook. In this case, you should meet together before starting the design to establish the basics for it. Team members can then complete their individual parts, and meet again to combine them.

Engage experts when needed (but don't assume they are always needed!)

While I maintain that anyone at any skill level can draw well enough to get basic points across visually, there are times when you will want a graphic designer or an artist to render the images for your designs. Likewise, you might need other professionals to help you write a scenario, or to assemble a complicated mockup. You will make the best use of your time and the time of your experts by understanding what you can do yourself. After you set tasks for yourself, you can determine exactly what you want from your professionals.

Save or Record Your Designs for Later Reference

Even if you believe your designs are expendable because, for instance, they are only an intermediate representation of your project, you will probably want to keep them around for later referral. This can be useful at later stages in the design process, when you are trying to remember why you made a certain decision or to help generate alternative ideas for concepts that did not work well. You also might need them to justify to others, such as your management or team members, why you made a particular decision.

You also might want to hold onto designs so that you can document the whole process, either to refer to when you have a similar task, or for publication of your findings in a technical journal. If you know from the onset of the design that these are possible concerns, choose off-line procedures that will best facilitate these goals.

Method 1: Off-line Design Materials

Any media that is appropriate for creating off-line designs of computer software, including paper, drawing utensils, cardboard, or plastics.

Let's start with the materials. I think it is important for people to realize the range available with which off-line designs can be created. The most conventional, and probably the ones you will use most often, are paper and pens of various weights and widths. Paper and pen are the most widely used for a number of reasons, the most obvious being that they are readily available and require no training to use. They are the perfect tools for creating many designs. Drawings and more complex paper-based designs such as storyboards and flipbooks can go a long way in communicating the features of a system or an application.

I always encourage designers to make use of materials that are readily available to them. Go through your desk or make a trip to the office stockroom to see what kinds of materials you have access to without having to make a special trip to the store. Self-adhesive notes in contrasting colors are great for illustrating parts of your scenario or storyboarding. They can be placed on larger pieces of paper, removed and rearranged without having to cut and paste images. They also are an excellent way to facilitate team designing: each team member can make illustrations, then the team can pick and choose among the illustrations to string together a design.

There will, of course, be times when the materials on hand are not enough for creating the designs you have in mind. Then it's time for a trip to an art supply store or a well-equipped office supply store. Browse before you select the materials you want, even if you have specific items in mind. You will often discover other materials that might suit your purpose even better. At the very least, you will see the range of media/materials available to you, and be better prepared to identify what you might need in your next off-line design project. The salespeople at these stores are excellent sources of information, as well. If you describe to them the types of materials you are looking for, or even the purpose of your project, they might have well-informed suggestions for appropriate materials.

As you spend more time creating off-line designs, you will acquire a preference for certain tools you like best, or that seem to best meet the needs of your design projects. You will be amazed at how few tools you need to create a range of interesting and provocative designs. Examine the designs of your colleagues to see the kinds of materials they use—you can learn a lot about what works well in off-line designs by viewing as many designs as possible. Ask your colleagues to identify tools or materials that are unfamiliar to you, have a joint design session, or swap tools.

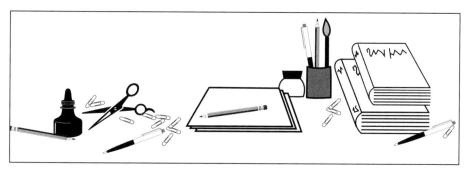

Figure 4.1 Illustration of Some Possible Materials. Materials themselves can be critical to the message delivered by your design. You can use a range of traditional artists supplies and techniques to create different designs which explore both the functionality and look of your emerging system.

The importance of materials

Selecting appropriate materials for your prototypes might not seem like a critical step in the software development process, but it can have significant impact on the designs you create. Some of the benefits of well-chosen materials are that they:

Help to communicate the design.

The materials used to develop off-line prototypes determine the aesthetic quality of those designs. They set the tone for the way those designs present their functionality and interactivity. While the designs themselves are the ultimate message, the materials are critical in communicating the designs.

Promote creativity and fun.

Different materials can encourage artistic capabilities and creative design. Choosing the right materials can help to promote innovation, and can actually make the difference in your approach to building an off-line prototype. With the appropriate materials, you will get your design ideas across, and have fun doing it.

Save you time.

Materials such as paper and pencil are extremely flexible and dynamic. They can be used in a variety of ways and can lead to a range of off-line prototypes. As a result, you will find that you are building more creative designs because you are not wasting time learning the intricacies of working with unknown tools or materials. Computer prototyping tools can be extremely restrictive in what they allow designers to create, whereas off-line prototypes can be anything the materials allow them to be.

Generate design ideas.

Looking for, and selecting, the materials you will use can actually help to generate ideas for your designs. Comparing your materials with others will help you with concepts and ideas that you might not otherwise have considered. Imagining ways in which you can use the various materials might help you to explore prototype functionality and purpose.

Require little overhead or investment.

The best thing about off-line prototype materials is that many of them are things you already have access to. This makes the whole process inexpensive. Even if you must obtain new or additional materials, the cost is relatively low, especially when compared to the cost of computer design tools or platforms.

Steps for gathering materials

1. Assess the needs of your design. If you will start with drawings, basic pencil and paper will probably be fine. If you want to build a more interactive prototype, you will need less conventional materials.

2. Determine what materials you have on hand.

3. Map the available materials to your needs.

4. Determine if there are any additional materials you need, and, if so, where you can obtain them. If you do not know the specific material you want, determine the characteristics that it should have.

5. Gather additional materials.

Hints/suggestions

• Store materials in a common place so you always know where to look.

• Always be on the lookout for new and interesting materials. You might discover perfect finds when cleaning out the garage, browsing at the mall, or observing the supplies used at your child's school.

• Keep a list of good sources of materials. The list can include local stores or the names of people who have good ideas about appropriate media to use for different design problems.

• Learn to make do with what you have or what you can get. Off-line designs are not about beautiful, polished drawings or models. Your designs should communicate your ideas and get the job done. The materials you use are secondary.

Exercise task

Gather materials that might be useful to you in designing the supermarket guide. Look to see what materials are immediately available. Collect the materials in an specific location, so that when the time comes to complete your designs, you have them available. Make a trip to a local design or office supply store to see what other kinds of materials you might purchase. Browse the aisles just to see what's there, or have a type of model in mind and look for materials you might use to build that model.

Method 2: Scenarios

A design concept—most often in writing and presented as a story—that usually includes a description of users, the task to be performed, and how the system will work to accomplish it.

Beginning a user interface design—thinking for the first time about how the software will work or look—is often the most difficult step in the entire design process. Many designers have difficulty knowing where to start. One of the best ways is to create a description or scenario of the way the software or user interface will be used. Storytelling is an ability that comes naturally to many people, and it is a low-pressure way to think about the system you want to design. Scenarios discussed among design team members can be written down to share with others later.

A scenario can be a "snapshot" of the system in use, or a more general description of the users and their goals, or the basic functions of the system. You decide how specific to be, depending on the needs of your project and how much you know about the design. A scenario should consider the general user interface, including the usefulness of the system, the environment the system will be in, and the tools for interaction (such as a mouse-driven personal computer, a touch-screen wall-mounted information system, or a phone-accessed audio system). Writing a scenario helps you think about all of these aspects of your user interface, and helps you answer some questions about your design. In many ways, writing a scenario is like writing a story about your users to help you to identify many of their characteristics.

Scenarios can be used in a number of different ways. You can write a scenario to describe your system, geared to lead you through your design process. Writing a scenario describing the current state of the technology, is particularly useful when you don't know much about what you want the new system to do (when user studies have not been done or have not been helpful in identifying design criteria). By writing a story about what currently exists, you can identify what doesn't work and generate alternative story lines that solve design problems. Scenarios can also be used to discuss far-out possibilities or future technologies. Write a description of the way this system might work far in the future. Even if it is not the system you will implement, it might help to give you ideas about what you will implement. Use the scenario as a creative tool for generating ideas.

Sometimes you will start the design process by writing a scenario, then find you want to generate some visual designs (drawings or storyboards) to help clarify some of the elements of the scenario. Once you have worked through the visuals, you might find that you need to go back to the scenario format, to again use a more general tool to work out some ideas. Scenarios can be useful in various parts of the design process because they allow you to use creative brainstorming free from any constraints that might be imposed by a visual representation.

When writing a scenario, it helps to be as complete as possible. You will refer to your scenario throughout development; looking back at your scenario helps to more clearly understand design goals and clarify design. At other times, referring to the scenario will help you to get a better idea of the general qualities of the user interface and give you additional ideas or options. Writing the whole story, when you create your scenario, will give you room to grow with the design, and potentially lead you to think of important issues that you might otherwise have missed.

The importance of scenarios

Scenarios are excellent design tools for a number of reasons. Storytelling is an easily adaptable way to integrate a process with which users are already familiar into user interface development. Some of the reasons scenarios are important to the design process are that they:

Start the ideas flowing.

Storytelling is a natural way to begin to think about an interactive process. Most of us are well versed in communicating through narrative, and are familiar with the process of scenario building/storytelling. Knowing how to tell stories, especially among a group or design team, can free you from the process enough to concentrate on the functionality and interactivity of the technology. When you don't know where to start with information you have gathered, or you aren't sure how to tackle the constraints you've encountered on a design, chances are writing a scenario will get the ideas flowing.

Help piece together aspects of the interface.

The different aspects of your user interface can be drawn together through various segments of your scenario. The scenario need not be complete at first, and can, instead, be snippets of stories explaining different pieces of the technology. You can go back later and connect these components by adding to your story.

Support creativity before committing the design to a more visually concrete format.

An important element of scenarios is that they are free form and leave quite a bit to the imagination. Even the most detailed scenario might be interpreted differently by different team members. The phenomenon is much the same as seeing a film made from a book you have read—you might have imagined the characters or locales in your mind to be quite different from those presented by the movie. The lack of commitment to a storyboard can be excellent for keeping you from having to make decisions about platform dependencies, or even about what the elements of the system look like. Scenarios let you focus on function and interaction in the early stages of design.

Allow all members of the design team to express themselves in a common way.

Since narration and storytelling are skills that most people are socialized to have, all the members of a design team probably will be able to express themselves through scenarios. This makes scenarios an excellent tool for team design, since no team member should be intimidated by lack of this design tool. All team members can take part in the verbal scenario, the writing of it, and the reading of it for evaluation purposes.

Doesn't have to be a graphical user interface.

There is nothing necessarily graphic about the user interfaces described through scenarios because scenarios are not tied to visual representations. Scenarios can be great for presenting audio user interfaces, or any other non-graphic interactive system. You can tell a story about almost anything.

Steps for writing scenarios

1. Identify a user and a task for your scenario, focusing on the technology you are developing.

2. Provide additional background information, such as location, time of day, the user's environment.

3. Write a story about the user and the technology. Describe the task the user is trying to do, and the way he or she goes about doing it.

4. Include any relevant information about other people. If the task requires more than one user, describe them all and their differences. If the outcome of the task affects others, say so.

5. Tell more about the technology than you intend to actually build. This leaves room for expansion and helps you to be more creative.

```
┌────────────────────────────────────────────────┐
│       Scenarios for Space Planning (A Study in 3D │
│              Furniture Manipulation)              │
│              Penny Bauersfeld                     │
│                April 1990                         │
│                                                   │
│   Three scenarios are provided to illustrate the need │
│   for a 3D manipulation space planning application for │
│   a variety of users.                             │
│                                                   │
│   Scenario 1:  Moving the Microwave               │
│                                                   │
│   Janet wants to free up some counter space in the │
│   kitchen.  She decides to put a shelf between two │
│   cabinets, making a cubby area just big enough to │
│   hold her microwave oven.  She can then put the   │
│   microwave in the cubby hole, and open up the counter │
│   space where the microwave used to be for other use. │
│                                                   │
│   To build the new cubby area, Janet measures the  │
│   opening and cuts the wood to size.  She then slides │
│   the shelf into place and nails it perpendicularly to │
│   the adjoining walls.                            │
│                                                   │
│   She then lifts the microwave off the countertop and │
│   pulls it toward her to bring it out from under a │
│   cabinet.  Once the microwave is clear of the     │
│   cabinet, Janet lifts it until it is directly in  │
│   front of the new cubby area and then fits it into │
│   the cubby hole by resting the back end of the    │
│   microwave on the shelf and pushing it into place. │
│                                                   │
│   Scenario 2:  Hanging a Picture                  │
│                                                   │
│   Sam wants to hang a picture above his bed.  He wants │
│   it to be centered on the wall relative to his bed, │
│   and to be centered between the top of his backboard │
│   and the ceiling.                                │
└────────────────────────────────────────────────┘
```

Figure 4.2 Scenario example These short scenarios describe
elementary manipulation of furnishings and home appliances.
They were used to help design an interactive 3D manipulation
scenarios. Even brief scenarios can be useful and helping design-

He locates the point at which to place the nail by
locating the appropriately centered point and then
off setting to account for the size of his picture
and the position of the hanging wire on the back of
the picture. He hammers the nail into the wall.
Sam then lifts the picture from where it rests
against a side wall. He carries it over to the bed,
lifts it until the wire clears the nail, and then
lowers the picture until it rests securely. He
slides the wire along the nail to properly center
the picture.

Scenario 3: Setting up the Conference Room

John is building a new conference room in his
office. He wants to set up the furniture and
equipment in it to make sure that everything is in
order.

John scatters the chairs around the room. He pulls
the projection screen down so that it is centered on
the far wall. He sets up the overhead projector at
the end of the table farthest from the screen. He
turns on the projector and puts a slide up.

John then proceeds to sit in each of the chairs to
insure that the view of the projection screen is
clear from each. He shuts the curtains and then
turns the lights on, and sits in each of the chairs
again. He moves chairs and recenters the conference
table in the room as necessary to provide adequate
views from each of the chairs.

ers to understand the current tasks and envision the interaction of
the future system. The complexity and length of scenarios depends
on the resources available to you and the nature of the project.

Hints/suggestions

- Don't get bogged down with details; keep your format loose and general.

- To help you get started, first brainstorm with others to verbally develop a scenario, Then split up and write down the details.

- Generate alternative scenario segments, if appropriate. You don't need to rewrite the entire scenario, only those segments with more than one story line.

Exercise task

Write a scenario describing the use of the supermarket guide. Base the description of the system on information you gathered in your early user research. Remember that writing a scenario is simply telling a story about the user and the system. Keep it general, but try to touch on critical elements of your system. Address the following elements in your scenario:

- Who is the primary user of this guide? Are there secondary users? Give relevant demographic information about the users of the guide.

- Where is the guide placed? What is its environment? How does this affect system usage?

- What is the basic service the system supplies? What kinds of things does the user expect to be able to do?

- What method of feedback is used to communicate information to the user?

- Is there any output of the system (sound, paper, or otherwise)? What might the user do with this output?

Method 3: Drawing

A sketch or illustration that presents an idea in a visual way.

Drawings are nothing new to design in general, although the role of drawing in user interface design is not always recognized. I present here the critical elements of drawings as they relate to user interface design.

By drawings, I mean images or illustrations drawn on paper with pencils, pens, or markers that are made by either an individual or a group. While the type of drawing I am describing for user interface design is typically made with conventional tools, drawings might also be created on a computer using on-line drawing tools. Keep in mind that the purpose of drawings in the early stages of off-line prototypes is to spend as little time as possible perfecting details. Focus instead on getting ideas across. Computer tools might be a hindrance rather than a help to many people. However, experienced computer artists might prefer to complete some drawings using on-line tools and still meet the criteria of drawings as off-line prototypes.

Drawings are excellent ways to present ideas, and can be as simple or as complex as desired. Drawing a concept is a sure way to capture an idea quickly, without having to dedicate time to learning how to express the idea in a new tool or style. Drawing is a skill that most people have and, while not all of us draw like Leonardo da Vinci, the purpose of drawing in off-line prototypes is not to create timeless masterpieces. The quality of the drawing is not the important issue.

Yes, some drawings will require more skilled artists. I am not arguing that drawing professionals are never needed, only that for most concept drawings they are not. For some drawings where finer details of a design are exhibited or for drawings that will be used for presentation purposes outside of the core design team, the skills of a professional artist might be needed. If a skilled artist is not directly available on the design team, you might want to bring one in for specific cases. If you find that you are developing the types of user interface software that require frequent involvement by drawing professionals, you might very well wish to bring on a skilled artist as a full-time, dedicated member of your design team. Your specific design needs will dictate your need for a talented artist. Still, all members of the design team should feel free to use drawings to communicate ideas and concepts, regardless of their skill level.

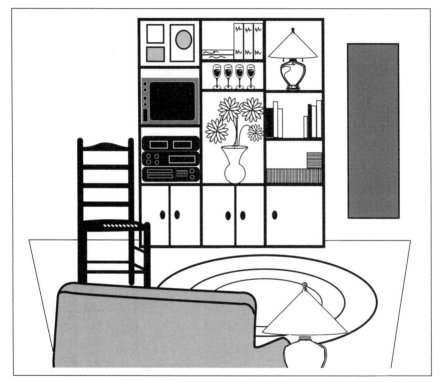

Figure 4.3 Drawing of a Living Room Environment. This sketch illustrates the A/V components and environment currently in the average living room - home entertainment system including television, stereo, VCR and speakers, and comfortably arranged furnishings. Using simple visual language to communicate the setting of today's or future technology can help you with your emerging design. Drawings don't have to be expertly rendered to communicate important information, in fact informal sketches can be more effective at illustrating the transient nature of early or evolving ideas.

Figure 4.4 Drawing of a Home Library. This drawing begins to scope out a possible front end for an on-line home library reference system. The looseness of the sketch captures an illustrative quality for the screen design, and the recognizable elements help to begin to piece together the interactive elements that might be presented as part of the user interface.

The importance of drawings

Drawings are an important off-line technique for designing user interfaces. Some of the reasons drawings are advantageous in this respect are that they:

Present ideas in a visual way.

Drawings are a transition from the words of your scenario to the visual expressions of your user interface software. They allow you to explore your design in greater detail, or to focus on a specific design element. Visual presentation of ideas is an important step toward clarifying the design—a picture is worth a thousand words.

Provide a common ground for group communication.

Since everyone on the design team can use this method to communicate, drawings can provide a common platform for participation. Even team members with no previous drawing experience can provide critical visual representations of their ideas and concepts using basic drawing techniques.

Are portable and easily reproducible.

Most drawings are created with paper and pencil, or other common materials. Thus, they can be created in many different environments, or started in one medium and revised in another. Drawings are easily reproducible (photocopied) and easily distributed among team members.

Can be embellished, if desired.

Drawings are easily updated or revised. Changes can be made with the same pen or pencil used on the original drawings. Parts of drawings can be copied over while changes are made in other parts, or additions can be made to an existing drawing. Possibilities abound for extending the use of drawings to later drawings that explore other ideas.

Can serve as the basis for later system components.

Drawings can be incorporated in later off-line prototypes, on-line prototypes, or even the final system, if appropriate. Even if they are not used directly in later designs, the concepts they present can be evolved into the later prototypes.

Steps for drawing

1. Identify critical ideas or concepts that require further thought or working through from a visual standpoint.

2. Gather appropriate materials for creating your drawings.

3.   Generate at least one drawing for each concept you want to illustrate.

4.   Use drawings in team meetings to express your ideas to your colleagues.

5.   Refine or revise drawings based on feedback from others and your own development.

6.   Use drawings in later designs, if appropriate.

Hints/suggestions

- Don't get caught up in the quality of the image. Start in and get your design across. You can revise the quality later if you feel it is appropriate.

- If you are apprehensive about your drawing abilities, practice. Doodles during meetings count! Or, if you are really nervous, take a one- or two-day drawing seminar.

- Develop a visual language you are familiar with one you can use repeatedly. In user interface design, finding standard representations for people, hands, computer hardware, and facial expressions is useful.

Exercise task

Draw some preliminary ideas for the supermarket guide. Some of the queries you might address with your drawings are:

- What does the guide look like (in a general sense)?

- Who are some of the people who might use the guide?

- What are some of the current information-gathering technologies?

- What are some of the elements in supermarket life? Consider produce, shelf products, check-out stands, supermarket personnel, coupons, flyers, and so forth.

Method 4: Storyboards

A sequence of drawings that tell a story about the user and the task to be accomplished by your system.

Storyboards take drawings one step further in explaining the user interface of your system. They present illustrations of key concepts from critical points of your scenario. They illustrate the current process that new technology will update, the new system, or a specific component of your system. No matter what the content of your storyboard, presenting additional information helps to refine and clarify the function or ease of use of your developing system.

The term storyboard comes from the film industry, where successive images are used to represent the overall storyline or plot. Storyboards are also used in animation to illustrate key segments of the story. Rectangular images or frames are laid out in a grid on a large piece of paper, one image per frame, with each image showing some evolution in the design. A line or two of text is usually written under each frame to define it. When you translate your scenario to visual form using storyboards, the text might actually come verbatim from your scenario.

Storyboards provide representational views of the user of the system, the task he or she is performing, and the environment in which it is performed. What you include in each frame depends on the nature of the design. Images can be substantially different from one another within a single storyboard sequence, as long as they illustrate key points in the design. In user interface software designs, you might design a storyboard that first illustrates the user with the machine in the designated environment, then a number of frames that show the user interacting with the machine or software, some frames depicting the changes in the software display as a result of a user action, and close with images of the effect the interaction has on the user or the environment.

While storyboards can show system functionality, the purpose of storyboarding is not solely to present linked screen shots of your potential system. Storyboards are most useful when they help to determine general factors in the interface, not simply what specific screens look like.

Figure 4.5 Storyboard template Creating and using a template for storyboarding can simplify your storyboarding process. This template shows a basic 6-frame layout, with space below each frame for textually describing the activity in the frame. Frames are small and probably appropriate for general or overview type storyboards which present basic concepts rather than system details. You may want to keep a number of different templates available so you can quickly duplicate the one most appropriate for your design.

Typically, a good way to develop storyboards is to take your scenario and identify the key segments or scenes. Select the scenes that describe important facts about the user, or the environment, or interaction with the system. Although developing storyboards need not follow writing scenarios, this sequence is a logical progression in your design process. Storyboards might also be appropriate at any time when features begin to surface that need visual design. You might find you get to on-line stages of development and are writing code when some aspect of the software is not clear. You can use storyboards at this point to flesh out an idea, or to communicate your design ideas to others. Storyboards are an excellent design tool because they combine narrative storytelling with visual representation of your design.

Figure 4.6 Sally in the morning storyboard This storyboard sequence chronicles the early morning life of Sally, a typical office worker. It maps out what Sally does in the morning before she goes to work, and before she takes advantage of any computing technology available to her in the office. It might be used to help understand where technology could be applied in the future, but is not taken advantage of today.

The importance of storyboards

Storyboards are useful design tools in many ways and can help you to:

Extend the verbal scenario to further explore the user interface design.

As storyboards are usually the next step after scenario development, they encourage you to extend your creative design process and further develop your user interface. Storyboards are a solid intermediate step in user interface design. Use them after you begin to understand the technology from the scenario, but before you have enough information to begin building the system on-line.

Begin to think about details of the interface.

Storyboards are often your first opportunity to start to think about visual details of the software—how it appears to the user, its look and feel, general layout issues, and so forth. It is a way to provide potential interface solutions through drawing. It can deliver a powerful message linking the elements of a scenario through pictures.

Illustrate ideas to designers and users.

Since storyboards get your ideas down on paper, you can use them as a communication tool. Show your storyboards to other members of your design team to promote group design and to encourage design efforts. Show your storyboards to potential users to get their reactions to the system design. An informational user study might be appropriate to gauge the success of the system based on the plans as presented by the storyboards.

Come to consensus as a team on critical feature and details.

Again, because storyboards can be used by all team members to express elements of the design, they can be excellent consensus-building tools for critical features or details. Different team members might sketch out their solutions to various problems as storyboard frames, and you can link appropriate frames together to arrive at a group design decision.

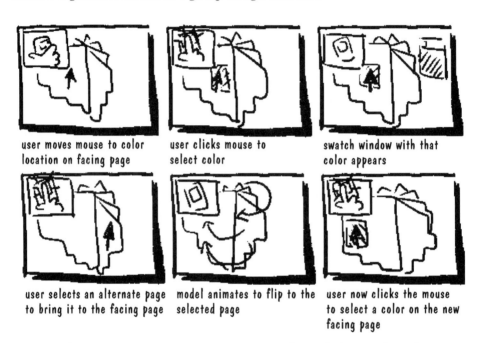

user moves mouse to color
location on facing page

user clicks mouse to
select color

swatch window with that
color appears

user selects an alternate page
to bring it to the facing page

model animates to flip to the
selected page

user now clicks the mouse
to select a color on the new
facing page

Figure 4.7 Mouse Interaction Storyboard This storyboard series illustrates an interactive sequence by showcasing user interaction with the mouse in the upper left corner of each frame. This series shows the design of a color selection system based on a three-dimensional color model. Depending on where the user clicks on the model, either a color is selected or the model rotates to support selection of an alternate set of colors. This type of interactive storyboard is useful in working out the user interaction of your system, both in terms of what the user can do and how the system responds.

Steps for storyboarding

1. Mark the key transitions, or critical points, in your scenario as key frames.

2. Draw a picture representing each of the key frames.

3. Draw the user, the system, or whatever else is important in this scenario. Some frames might show the entire environment, others might only show a computer screen.

4. Use a simple graphic language and repetitive symbols throughout the storyboards. For instance, use a hand in a bubble to indicate when the user must select something.

5. Write a short description of each frame explaining what is going on, or to describe the transition from one frame to the next. Be sure to describe non-graphic effects or interactions.

Hints/suggestions

- First draw a template for the frames. You might want to make several copies of this template, then simply fill in the illustrations for the storyboards.

- Consider using self-adhesive notes as the frames of your storyboards. They make it easy to reorder the frames, or to insert new ideas or remove old ones (without having to cut or redraw images on a single piece of paper). They are also an excellent way to design as a team, since individual team members can draw frames and then the group can string them together on a tabletop, wall, or large sheet of paper.

- Use a copy machine to duplicate repetitive parts so you don't have to redraw the same image.. This is especially useful for storyboards that show changes in a user interface that have a common background.

Existing Button Metaphor - Simple Go & Return Screen

Alternak Metaphor - Simple Go & Return Screen

Alternate Metaphor - Entry Screen (Shows up after preliminary info gathering)

Figure 4.8 Travel request storyboard alternatives These storyboards show some alternative designs for an on-line system for making travel arrangements developed by the Stanford University Data Center. The first storyboard presents the current design, with interactive buttons along the bottom for selecting which type of travel information to enter. The second storyboard shows an alternative, where information types are presented as a file folder model across the top of the screen. The third design illustrates a less structured approach, based on a travel agent's model of presenting pamphlets providing the various services typically required for travel arrangements.

Exercise task

- Design and create a storyboard to illustrate your supermarket guide scenario. Identify the key frames of the scenario and create an illustration for each of them. Where appropriate, point out user interaction. Be sure that you:

- Provide initial and final frames that are general in nature, and that present the user, the guide, and the overall environment.

- Illustrate what is going on with the system, as well as the user's reaction to various activities. Use facial expressions to represent the user's reaction.

- Incorporate elements of your preliminary drawings. While your drawings were not as directed as your storyboards should be, there might be elements elements you can reuse.

- Start to really think about your system. While storyboards generally follow your scenario, there is plenty of room to be creative with design alternatives.

- Develop alternative frames or even entire storyboards for ideas that you believe deserve consideration. Encourage input from others, and feel free to change your frames or suggest alternatives whenever you feel the need.

Method 5: Flipbooks

Visual representation of the system and the interaction that makes it function, usually screen shots linked together by user input.

In order for your prototypes to start to approximate the final system, they should begin incorporating some interactive behavior of the on-line application. Flipbooks are a way to design a more concrete representation of your system and to add interaction to your drawings and storyboards, mapping potential user input to system responses. Typically, flipbooks are paper and pencil images arranged in like a stack of paper each page representing a snapshot of the computer screen. Interaction is demonstrated by linking interactions on pages of the flipbook, with button selections or clicking choices, to another page. While all interactions in your final system may not be so absolute, you can use a flipbook to approximate them and begin to map out your system. You can present flipbooks to users to obtain feedback on system design.

In building a flipbook, you can begin to design and explore your overall system. and translate system features to actual functions in the system. While you need not represent every function of your system in your flipbook, it is a good idea to include as many as possible. Flipbooks support testing of system functionality off-line, without having to design the underlying code to support a working system. Indeed, you can try out alternative interactions, multiple options for pages in the flipbook, and substitute one page for another to observe the interactions.

Flipbooks are not simply the stacking of storyboards together. The intention is to have the pages of the flipbook look as close as possible to the final computer screens. Storyboards, on the other hand, include either textual or visual information about the entire system, the environment, or the reasoning behind the design.. A flipbook does not include any such information. Storyboards tell a story, and are communicative tools used to inform design team members. Flipbooks, instead, mime the actual system in detail.

In building a flipbook, think about the overall structure of your system perhaps drawing out a system map, a hierarchical representation of the screens or elements of your system. Where a hierarchical representation is possible draw out small graphic representations of your screen images and link them together using a linear tree model. A line from one screen representation to another when it is possible to go to that screen from the first screen should be represented as an interaction and supported in your flipbook.

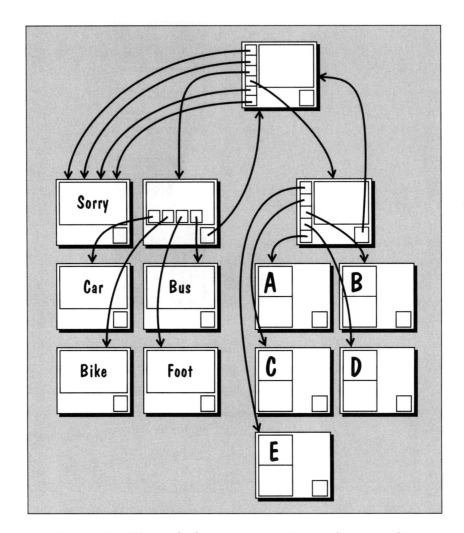

Figure 4.9 Hierarchal system map Using a basic graphic language to describe the overall hierarchy of your system can be helpful in understanding interaction and navigation. This illustration of a system may shows how the layout the relation of various interactive elements and screens can be used to examine system movement. You can look for consistency of interaction, completeness of the interface, and balance of the system.

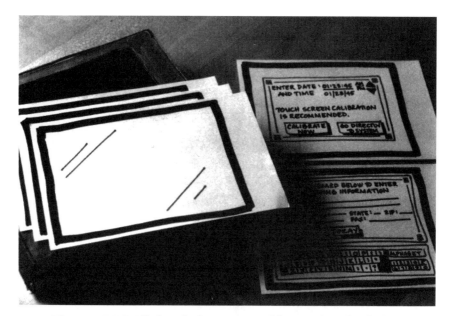

Figure 4.10 Flipbook for a Portable Device This flipbook
illustrates a user interface for a small hand-held computing device.
A foam core model was built to represent the device and house
the interactive flipbook. Screen shots are represented on individual index cards, which can be fitted into the screen region of the
model. Cards are "flipped" according to user interaction with the
card currently showing.

It is important to remember that you do not want your interactive features
to be any more visible in your flipbooks than they will be in your final system. This is particularly important if you plan to use a flipbook to perform
user studies of your system's interaction. Instead of labeling the interactive
moves in the flipbook itself, you can use various tactics to keep track of the
interaction without presenting it to the users. One way to do this is to keep
a written account of the results of any interaction on a separate sheet of paper,
or simply number the pages.. Then, for each page in the flipbook keep track
of what page to turn to according to what user action is taken. You might
want to note these potential interactive moves on the back of each flipbook

page, localizing the information , or incorporate it into the design by, say, having liftable tabs revealing where to go upon selection. Use tabs that will not draw undue attention to buttons or other elements, if you don't you will only stall the identification of problems with your user interface later on by not being true to your system in this important off-line design phase.

Because storyboards are visual representations of your system, you should design some storyboards before you go on to design and build a flipbook. This will allow you to take advantage of visual elements addressed in your storyboards when you design your flipbooks. You may find you need to think about interactivity quite a bit before you can come up with the final interactive flipbook design, and working with a flipbook will help you to identify much of this interaction this because the page-by-page off-line design of a flipbook supports your conceptualizing. And like other off-line designs, it supports team design, as various team members might develop individual screens or flipbook pages. You will almost always benefit by developing a flipbook before an actual system, even if you don't use it to test users. In the long run, developing a flipbook can identify and solve problems and inconsistencies with your system before you have invested time in on-line development.

Flipbooks are perhaps the most important of off-line prototypes you can develop because for users they are an approximation of the final system and can be used to gain feedback on the system's design. While other off-line designs help you to understand critical elements of the system to be incorporated into your flipbook designs, only flipbooks let you explore elements of the entire system. Some of the reasons flipbooks are most important are that they help you to:

- Understand the extent and scope of your system: Using a flipbook to develop system interaction will help you better understand the scope and structure of the entire system, even if you don't develop a flipbook that includes every screen or every interactive move of your system. You can follow interactive paths all the way through the system, and see repeated patterns of interaction that occur throughout.

- Identify the role of each function and interaction in relation to all others: Building a flipbook and using it to approximate system interaction will help you to see how various functions in your system interrelate. You can scope out interactive inconsistencies, and build a more dynamic and successful system in doing so.

- Test a system's usability before committing to working prototypes: Flipbooks allow you to come close to system functionality without having to actually build anything on-line. They are close enough to the real thing, so much so, that you can get amazingly significant feedback on system usability through user testing flipbooks. Usability studies of flipbooks can help you to identify large or general difficulties with your system, which you can then correct and retest before committing to anything on-line. Designing, building and testing interactive flipbooks are an excellent technique for user interface design.

Hints/Suggestions

- Use your storyboards as a starting point for your visual screen representations. Even if your storyboards do not clearly represent screen shots of the system, they include important information about what should be included.

- Use already bound materials, such as a spiral notebook or pad of notecards, to hold your flipbook. You may want to design portions of the flipbook separately, then make a final version using such materials.

- As with storyboards, use a copy machine or post-it notes if appropriate.

- Don't feel like you have to develop the whole system in a flipbook before presenting it to users. If you are at a point where critical user input might be helpful, show a partial flip-book during user studies.

- See Chapter 7 on User Testing to better understand how your usability studies might be conducted and to help you in design your flipbook to best meet your study needs.

Exercise

- Design and build a flipbook for your supermarket guide. If time permits, and you have access to potential users, show the flipbook to some of them to get feedback on system inter-action. Developing the flipbook will require you to explore some of the physical elements of your system. Some of the things you will want to consider in designing your flipbook are:

- How large should your "pages" be? If you are designing a large screen on-line guide, you will want to use large sheets of paper. If the screens are to be small, index cards may be better suited.

- Will you use color or black-and-white images? You will prob-ably want to be as true to the final designs as possible.

- How will your flipbook images change from your storyboards? What information will you want to omit, or develop further?

- Design multiple options for certain interactions? Designing more than one possibility and then reviewing them side-by-side might help you choose the best one for your flipbook.

- How will you label the pages of your flipbook and represent the interaction? Will numbering be appropriate, or labeling the pages "Main menu", "Dairy section", etc. be a better method

- How will you "run" your flipbook? When you present your flipbook to potential users to explore system usability, will you have smooth interactions (so as not to distract the user from the tasks at hand) or will you allow the user to see the methods for maneuvering the flipbook.

Method 6: Mockups

Physical model of a system and its user interface illustrating interactive elements of the system, incorporating a flipbook or other off-line interactive design.

Some systems involve special hardware or a novel use of the device which may critically affect the user interface. While the off-line prototyping techniques described above can be helpful in designing these systems as well, building a physical model or mockup of the system may be an important aid in developing the interactive technology. In systems where hardware interaction is critical, such as button pushing or highlighted choices on the frame of a device, mockups allow you to explore user reaction to these important elements.

A mockup can be built from any combination of materials you believe are appropriate. Some that you might find most useful are cardboard, foamcore, masonite or plastics. The intent of a mockup is to represent the final system not build a true representation of the final system. . A mockup should readily present system functionality and layout being a substitute for the real thing allowing observation of interaction and functionality without spending the time to build the real system. A mockup-flipbook integrated system can be particularly useful for usability studies when a new type of hardware is planned A mockup incorporating an index card flipbook, lends itself particularly well to test users' reactions to system interactions, as well as to the overall system.

The Importance of Mockups

While building a mockup is not critical to the design process for each and every application or system, it can be a useful technique for certain systems, particularly those that depend on novel hardware interactions. Some of the reasons it might be advantageous to develop a mockup is that mockups can:

- Support exploration of physical characteristics that paper alone could not.

- Give clues as to interaction between software and hardware.

- Allow you to test additional elements of a system without building the real thing.

- Provide additional criteria for usability evaluation.

Steps for Building Mockups

1. Identify and gather appropriate materials.

2. Decide if you will incorporate a flipbook in the design. If so, at least start to design the flipbook so that you have enough of it to insure it is sized appropriately.

3. Design the mockup, thinking about how you will use your materials. Careful design can   help you avoid wasted time or supplies.

4. Build the mockup.

5. Test your mockup, making sure components are sturdy enough to withstand any usage or testing you plan.

6. Complete the flipbook component if you have included one (and not already done so).

Hints/Suggestions

- Make use of available materials.

- Take advantage of materials with which you already know how to work. Again, the purpose of a mockup is not to actually build a working system, but to quickly and efficiently explore the physical elements of your design. Using materials you can readily manipulate is a definite plus.

- Consider the purpose of the mockup before you build it. Focus on the elements that are important to your exploration, not necessarily every detail of the system.

Exercise

- If your design for your supermarket guide entails physical elements in the user interface design a mockup of the system. Remember that the mockup should focus on the elements of the system which might not otherwise be evident in the paper prototypes of your storyboards or flipbook. In designing the mockup, you will want to think about:

- Identifying the particular interactive elements first, so that you can focus on them as the critical elements of your mockup—such as certain push buttons.

- Incorporating the flipbook you designed for the last exercise. Even if it is not true to size or form, for the purpose of this exercise it may serve well enough.

- Knowing that you will use the mockup as a test piece before you build it may affect the way you build it.

Chapter 5

On-line Tools and Procedures

What Are On-line Tools and Procedures?

Early user studies and off-line prototypes are excellent ways to take advantage of non-computer techniques to help you better visualize and understand your designs. However, you are building a software application or system, and at some point your design will need to address the many issues involved with taking it on-line. While it can incorporate many off-line methodologies, a successful software design ultimately depends on the computer platform. Many on-line tools and procedures are available to you to continue your design process and to address the on-line elements of your software. This chapter presents some of the techniques for using on-line tools and procedures in developing both prototypes for your system or application, as well as for building the system itself.

Before you build the actual system, you should design and build on-line prototypes to help address the technology-based issues of your software. Think of them as the beginning of your on-line designs, though they might not actually evolve into your final system. On-line prototypes should be considered as disposable as your off-line prototypes—if they do not meet system needs, don't incorporate them simply because they exist. You will probably be able to use elements of your prototypes, but if you allow for disposability from the beginning, you will protect yourself from potentially damaging decisions later on.

You can use on-line prototyping and techniques to work on many aspects of your system that were hypothetical until this stage of development:

- Experimenting with certain physical components, such as screen size and input device interaction.

- Determining the appropriate software platform.

- Testing development tools.

- Testing existing modules that might be included in the final program.

- Identifying system speed and memory requirements (or constraints).

- Determining program size and storage requirements (or constraints).

- Experimenting with image and sound data access and storage and performance.

These issues cannot be addressed in the early concept phases of design (nor should they be). By moving your design process on-line, you can begin to deal with the technology-dependent aspects of your design and understand the effects as you develop your system.

Your on-line prototyes might not be developed on the hardware platform of your final product. You might not have access for testing purposes to the hardware or software that you will use ultimately. You might not even know the target hardware or software platform! On-line design can help you to identify the appropriate platform.

Before deciding which platform to use for this stage of development, ask yourself this question: What is the purpose of this on-line prototype? If it is for testing interactivity during user studies, then the exact platform is not critical. It is more important to pick a platform with familiar software prototyping tools so you can quickly mockup your designs and get necessary feedback. If, on the other hand, you are trying to understand specific hardware constraints and how they affect the design, then you should use the hardware the final system will use. You might want to develop different designs on alternate platforms—the decision is up to you. The specifics of your design problem will help lead you to the appropriate hardware or software for on-line design.

On-line designs are useful for obtaining user feedback. Presenting users with "working" computer-based versions helps you identify some of the critical issues of a system. For example, suppose you are trying to decide on the balance to strike between image quality and program speed. You could develop several prototypes, each representing a different balance between the two. Present the prototypes to potential users. Use their feedback to help you reach a decision. On-line designs that illustrate various options are effective decision-making tools.

On-line designs are typically developed after off-line designs. This is because off-line designs are most effective for getting at the large issues and elements of the user interface. Time spent developing off-line designs saves you time with on-line designs. However, computer-based designs might be developed simultaneously with off-line designs, particularly if potential problems or system constraints are known. This is an excellent approach when you are lucky enough to be part of an interdisciplinary team where visual designers are working on the overall design, and software engineers are addressing some of the known on-line issues. Typically such early on-line designs gather information or evaluate options, and later on-line designs incorporate the efforts from the user studies and off-line designs.

The Advantages of On-line Tools and Procedures

Your on-line designs are the basis for your user interface software. They are important in the overall development process because they:

Help you prepare for the real system.

On-line designs help you learn about and structure the design for your final software application or system. They introduce you to the issues you will face in implementation and give you some experience working on a potential, or known, platform. Moving your designs on-line will prepare you for actual system development.

Start the software development phase.

While off-line research and prototyping are valuable to the development process, at some point you do have to write the software. Taking advantage of on-line tools and procedures helps you start on your software, without the worry that you aren't ready to build the real thing. On-line designing and prototyping will help you make the transition to building your software application or system.

Promote rapid prototyping with extension possibilities.

Approaching your on-line designs as part of the overall design process can help you accomplish rapid prototyping techniques, rather than belaboring the details of the intended software development. It helps to think of your software elements as modular and reusable, since you will probably want to extract portions for inclusion in other projects.

Begin the transition from off-line designs.

On-line designs are a logical next step for your off-line designs. While you probably could prototype off-line for more time than is typically given, there comes a time when you have issues and questions that can be addressed only by developing on-line work. On-line tools and procedures help you through the transition from the off-line designs and their related issues to an on-line format that paves the way for the final software.

Provide a more realistic platform for user studies and tests.

While you can learn a significant amount about a system by conducting user studies with off-line prototypes, sometimes certain feedback can only be attained with an on-line piece. Depending on the nature of the software under development, users might need to see parts of it running on a plausible hardware platform to envision how it will work, or what it will do for them. Moving your designs on-line will provide you with a more realistic test of your software with potential users.

Point out potential system constraints.

Working on-line helps you resolve the issues introduced in your off-line work, and might reveal additional issues or constraints not dealt with earlier. Working on-line will be a better representation of the nature of the final software, pointing out issues such as screen size or resolution, input device abilities, storage or memory limitation, or other physically binding elements not considered when you were working off-line.

How to Select, Design and Perform On-line Tools and Procedures

The criteria for selecting and applying on-line tools and procedures are similar to those for off-line tools and procedures. They are, after all, used for similar purposes—to design and develop your software system. As with off-line tools, it might seem difficult at first to decide which on-line tools to use when developing your designs. With time, you will simply know from the nature of your design problem which techniques are appropriate. Follow these guidelines when making your decisions:

Determine how much time you have in your schedule.

As with so many design techniques, time is probably your most significant factor in identifying the methods that will work best for your design problem. Unfortunately, project schedules and deadlines will often dictate the techniques used. Work backwards from known deadlines, estimating how much time you will be able to spend on developing your on-line designs. Estimate the amount of time required for the various techniques you will apply to your design problem.

Once you know your time limitations, you can look for problems or issues you know you must address with on-line designs. Allocate time for these types of design pieces first. If you still have additional time, then you can assess if other methodologies will be useful, and which ones to apply.

Look at what you already know about constraints or potential problems.

Major issues for on-line prototyping are often identified in earlier development stages or even known from the start. Such issues might include whether or not users can successfully manipulate a targeted interactive device, or if an intended software development environment can support the range of bitmap images that will be necessary to implement your targeted design. Being aware of these constraints from the start can help you decide how to apply various on-line techniques. You might need to conduct some early on-line studies to evaluate whether the given constraints are truly a problem for your design, or you might look for available clip art if you know you need to generate a high number of on-line images. While constraints are perceived as negative limitations on your range of design options, they often wind up helping you make decisions in your overall process.

Assess the equipment and tools available to you.

On-line designs give you an opportunity to assess the equipment and tools you will use and to evaluate hardware issues. Once you know the hardware and software you will use for your development, you can evaluate equipment for how it meets your needs and then apply techniques on that platform to determine the specifics of your design.

If you are choosing from a variety of available platforms, on-line designs can help you to compare the various platforms, evaluating which one best meets your needs. As you evaluate the hardware, you might identify problems or constraints that help to make your decision clear. Spending time early on comparing the equipment options could save you significant time later by helping you to avoid an inappropriate platform for your design.

Assess what you have learned from off-line prototypes.

Your earlier off-line designs will often indicate problems or questions that can be addressed only with on-line designs. Earlier work might point out the need for representing visual images on-line, or testing actual components of the system, or evaluating whether or not a video segment can be interrupted and reset in real time.

Even if your off-line designs did not suggest obvious areas for on-line work, you might go back over your designs or notes and reevaluate whether or not anything there readily lends itself to an on-line prototype. You might find that certain elements of the system can now be designed, built, and evaluated once you move your development on-line.

Take into account what you have learned from user studies.

As with earlier off-line designs, early user studies provide obvious indications of the types of designs you want to conduct on-line. Sometimes your users will ask you directly if something will be implemented in a certain way, or point out areas where details have not been provided and will need to be before the final software can be built. (Be sure to make note of these issues during your studies, since they will be valuable in helping you during on-line prototyping.)

Even when users are not so direct in their feedback, they can lead you to these problem areas. Evaluate user performance, asking yourself what kinds of on-line work are appropriate. Often in assessing early user studies, you will find indications of what issues should be addressed by an on-line study.

Evaluate the purpose of your designs.

Ask yourself from the beginning what you hope to accomplish with your on-line designs.

If you are building on-line designs to test implementation details—such as the capabilities of a certain software development environment, or whether or not you can successfully play sound or video from within your application—then you will not have to worry about the visual details of this on-line piece.

If you are designing a backbone or some other module of code that might be adapted into a future prototype or into the final system, then spend a little more time structuring your code and document it accordingly. Documenting the code is important, whether or not you intend to share the code with other development team members. (We all can forget why we did something a certain way, particularly if it's been some time since we looked at the code.)

If your designs will be used in user studies to provide additional feedback for development, then you have additional requirements to consider. You might need to include more accurate visuals, or implement an interactive driver if people will actually work with your piece during the user studies. Understanding what you will do with your on-line designs will dictate the methodologies that will work best for developing the on-line design.

Consider what might be translated to the final system.

Off-line prototypes, while they might show you important facts about your design, can not be directly incorporated into final working software. On-line designs can be, when appropriate. The danger with on-line designs is that part or all of them will be directly incorporated into the final software simply because they are there. You can save yourself valuable development time by asking, before you create an on-line prototype, if the form and function you envision will be truly useful. If the response is no, or even a weak yes, then reevaluate your prototype design. Knowing helps to steer you toward, or away from, certain on-line methods.

Method 1: Early On-line Explorations

Studies built with prototyping tools or simple code sequences that examine the different components that make up a system.

Begin your on-line designs with short, simple modules of code that test a potential system feature, or that allow you to write a function in a particular development environment. This piece of code does not need to be a part of your final software application or system. It might serve no purpose other than to give you practice writing code in this language or environment. However, the importance of the code is that it plays a necessary role in your software development. These segments of code are referred to as early on-line explorations.

Early on-line explorations are open-ended in nature, and can be any early piece of code that helps in your on-line development. For example, you might write code for reading and interpreting input from a particular input device, or for accessing video drivers. You might use on-line explorations to translate off-line designs to an on-line form. This could involve scanning in visuals you used in an off-line prototype and representing them in a target software environment. Or it might mean that you implement a proposed interactive module to see if it can actually work in your on-line system. No matter what way you find it appropriate to convert your off-line designs, they can be an excellent indication of the early work you will want to do on-line.

Early on-line prototypes do not have to wait for finalized off-line designs to get started. On the contrary, they might even begin before off-line designs begin, particularly if known issues limit the capabilities of your on-line designs. For instance, if you are unsure whether or not your platform will be able to support color software, limiting you to black and white designs, you might want to check whether or not color is feasible. The result should direct the use of color or black and white only in your off-line designs. As soon as potential platforms and technologies have been identified, you will want to start your on-line design process.

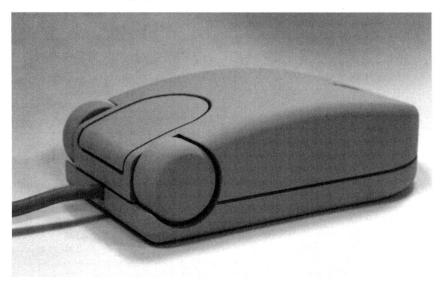

Figure 5.1 Early on-line prototype hardware. When new or exploratory input devices are used, it is probably a good idea to build an early on-line prototype. This photo of a thumbwheel mouse (developed by Dan Venolia of Apple Computer) is an example of such a prototype input device. It is a standard computer mouse with a roller wheel. Early on-line prototypes can help both to test the device drivers themselves to be sure the input device functions properly and to begin to try out possible interpretations of interactive behavior.

On-line explorations are appropriate during the course of either early user research or off-line prototyping. When either of these activities introduces issues critical to your on-line system, conduct an on-line project that addresses them. On-line designs resolve these issues and make your off-line process more accurate. They also might suggest a solution that was not apparent in the off-line design phaze. Performing on-line explorations in conjunction with other design development enables you to incorporate early findings into your software, too. Depending on the nature of your project, you might choose not to turn to on-line procedures until you obtain some results from early studies and off-line work.

Early on-line explorations should begin before any actual design, but these explorations need not be limited to a particular stage of development. They might be appropriate any time an implementation or software function question arises—something software developers know can happen at any point in the design process. Additionally, short on-line explorations can be valuable for testing projected useability. The nature of your design problem will help you to see where on-line explorations can be used best.

The importance of early on-line explorations

Early on-line explorations support critical efforts in the software development process because they give you hands-on experience with the software itself. They are important to the overall design process because they let you:

Test feasibility before making a major investment in a technology.

On-line explorations allow you to quickly and simply evaluate singular parts of the system without having to build the whole thing. It makes much more sense to complete a short development task that might help you resolve issues or problems with your system than to try to isolate that problem within the context of your entire program. Early on-line designs can often help you evaluate whether certain software or hardware systems are appropriate for your design. They can save you from making a mistake in adopting a specific platform without knowing how it will handle some issues that are critical for your design.

Reduce on-line time and effort.

Probably the best reason to conduct early on-line explorations is to save yourself time and trouble later. While at first it might seem like it takes added time to conduct the early work, this early work typically answers questions and makes less work overall. This is particularly true when you find yourself incorporating the early explorations into later software. When you already know that the software supports the function for which it is designed and that the function is appropriate for the environment, you can quickly integrate that portion of the program into the final product, saving time in the long run.

Allow the software engineer to begin working while waiting for the results of early users tests and off-line design evaluations.

Earlier chapters advocate conducting research and building off-line designs before the actual software development starts. Note that this is the actual software development, not any software development. You can begin early on-line designs as soon as software issues are identified, or when you realize that implementing some on-line designs might help direct user studies or off-line prototyping. Early on-line designs help the software engineer get involved with software design without writing the actual code (which could potentially limit design options in the long run).

Compare implementation on various platforms and identify the appropriate platform for actual development.

One useful activity a software engineer can perform in early on-line designs is evaluating the platform for development. If potential platforms are known, on-line explorations might be devised that help to compare one platform to another. These pieces enable the software engineer to make valuable contributions to the overall development activity, and to prepare for both the development of further prototypes and the final system.

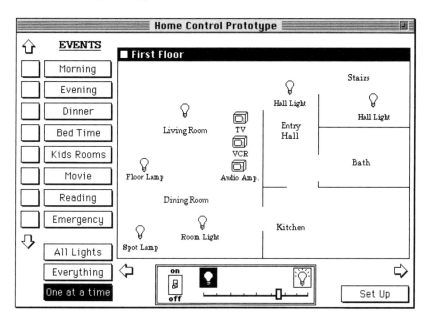

Figure 5.2 Early on-line prototype for the home control stack. This HyperCard stack was created early in the development process of a remote control application for accessing various home electronic devices. While not pretty to look at, it shows access to the main functions projected to be important to the system. This basic interface was not intended to be shown to users, but rather to test technical feasibility of accessing these features from a HyperCard stack. Early on-line prototypes such as these enable you to confirm that you can accomplish the basic tasks of your system. Your success (or failure) may help influence the design of your system.

Steps for performing early on-line explorations

1. Write a code module in the targeted language or software environment. Build a piece of code that addresses some known problem, or will be incorporated later.

2. Practice input and output routines on target hardware. If visuals will be displayed on a graphic screen, begin to understand display requirements. If user input will be with a mouse, understand event dynamics by writing a short sample program to read mouse input.

3. Identify inter-dependencies by separating logical components of the software. Understand how various modules will need to communicate.

4. Build small applications or subsets of the type of application to be built. Sample applications allow the exploration of various components without building a larger scale system.

Hints/suggestions

• Build many small prototypes rather than one large one, with each small prototype dedicated to a specific technology or feature. Your findings, from these small component-based prototypes, will be easier to incorporate into your future system.

• Take advantage of early on-line prototypes to test out potential hardware or software novelties. This is your opportunity to see how the technology might work for you or against you. It is to your advantage to find out as early as possible if there will be problems in your system development, and to communicate them to other team members.

- Communicate with other team members who are conducting early user studies or developing on-line prototypes to see if they are counting on certain technologies. These might be the technologies you want to explore with your early on-line prototypes.

- If you have extra time in these early stages (while waiting for results from early studies or other prototypes), spend some time exploring system extensions or alternatives. They might prove handy later.

Exercise task

Think about, plan, and implement at least one early on-line prototype for your supermarket guide. Consider experimenting with potential input or output devices, or software models of interaction. Before you begin to build anything, spend some time organizing your thoughts on what will work best for you. Some things to consider are:

- Is there any hardware with which you are unfamiliar and that you should test? If so, a prototype involving such hardware would be a good candidate.

- Do you know of any particular software necessary to support your system? If so, a prototype involving this software might prove useful. If not, you might design a small test prototype that you can try on a range of software platforms that are available to you, and use this prototyping stage to evaluate your options.

- What can you learn from designing and building this early prototype that will help you later on?

- What are the implementation details—size, memory, cost, time? If they are factors in your prototype, then they will be factors in the development of your target system.

Method 2: System Requirements

Explanation of the needs of the system from the engineers or programmer's point of view.

Early in the development of the software itself, you should write a plan of action that explains what the system will do and how it will do it. This is the system requirements document. It does not need to be long or formal, just a simple description of the system that can serve as a reference, and as a basis for further work for the system engineers or programmers. A useful system requirements document could be anywhere from two pages to one hundred, depending on your system and how you work as a software developer. Overall, system requirements should present the information telling you what you need to build the system.

Many companies and organizations have a process in place for software development that includes system requirements documentation. If yours is one of them, you could address the issue of a system requirements document by completing your company's standard working procedures.

Whether you use a documentation procedure already in place, or devise one yourself, remember that the purpose is not to meet some company policy. It is to help you prepare for the implementation of your system, and to lay out a plan for software development. It should help you better understand any hardware or software platform requirements or constraints, and give you some idea of how individual elements of the system will work, as well as a picture of the whole system working together. It will help you answer some of the questions necessary before development can continue, and indicate other areas where further development or research might be necessary. If your company's documentation process does not address these issues, then it is in your best interest to take a bit of extra time to draft a system requirements document that will suit your needs.

Writing the system requirements documentation

While there is no precise formula for writing system requirements, there are a number of elements that you will probably address for any application or system you are developing.

Implementation issues.

Address implementation issues specific to running on the intended hardware or software. If you do not know at the time of writing of the system requirements what either the hardware or software will be, then you can use the requirements document to list known characteristics of the target platform. Completing the systems requirements as an exercise might help you determine either your hardware or software platform, or at least narrow your search by having you think about these very real system development issues.

System components.

Analyze the components of your system. With as much detail as you can, tell about what each module of the software will do, how they will link together, and which parts of the software are necessary for user interaction.

Audience for the documentation.

Think of writing the system requirements as drafting a contract for what you will be building. Depending on any company policy you might have in place or on the size of your design team, others might write the document with you or be part of the target audience. Clearly, however, as system implementor, you are (at least one of) the target audience for your system requirements document. You will refer to it to see what you had in mind for implementation throughout the development process.

Structured development plan.

While it might evolve as your work continues, you should use your requirements document as a structured basis for system development. If your requirements change, change the document, even if only informally scribbling on it. This way, you will be able to track the development process. Using the system requirements document as a structured plan can help you to best organize your implementation process and proceed in a logical and efficient way.

How to use the system requirements documentation

You probably learned about system requirements, as it is presented here, in a software engineering program at school, or you might find that it is similar to processes that are in place at your work. You will probably find that the document itself is similar to other documents with which you are familiar. The primary difference, however, is the role it plays in system development. Write a system requirements document after early design and development have clearly indicated system needs. Start with the user needs that arise from research and the designs evolved during earlier prototyping stages. Once your basic user requirements are known, then write the system requirements document to insure that the system you develop meets these design criteria.

In traditional software engineering programs, software developers are taught to write system requirements at the very beginning of the development process. In practice, this forces you to develop a system that addresses only what is known about hardware and software at the time the project begins. This can severely cripple your ability to address user needs.

While you might draft your system requirements before you begin building your system, which will save hack time later, recognize that there is a lot of design and prototyping work that will go on before you implement the system. You should elaborate on and refine the document after design and prototyping provides significant information about the nature of the system. Remember to revise your system requirements to reflect changes in the design that develop as you begin to implement the actual system or as further research or design work indicates a need for change. Looking at the system requirements as an informal but influential part of the overall design process will help you to best use them to meet your needs.

The importance of system requirements

System requirements documentation is important to the system implementor for many reasons. Some of the most important are that they help you to:

Understand the system better in early stages.

Even if you believe you have carefully thought out many aspects of the system you are developing, writing down your thoughts will almost always help you to find inconsistencies or design flaws. It is extremely important that you understand your system implementation and the structural decisions you have made at the very early phases. As your system develops and gets more complex, your design structuring problem only continues to grow. When you use system requirements documentation to understand your system's functionality and implementation early on, you set a strong guide for further development work.

Document a development plan for referral later.

Writing down your system implementation plan at the beginning of your development process gives you a point of reference. You can turn back to your documentation to recall what you intended to do with your design, or why you chose an initial underlying structure. The document preserves your thoughts, helping you to decide later if you are adhering to the plan or if you should revise the design.

Make an agreement among implementors.

If your implementation will be done by more than one person, then you should draft the system requirements document as a sort of contract among implementors. Different team members might contribute different sections of the requirements document, describing the parts they will be building. Even if only one person writes the document, team members can agree to the final version and work together to keep the document current as the system implementation progresses.

Home Control System
Preliminary System Requirements
Penny Bauersfeld
February 1, 1990

OVERVIEW This document describes a system for
control of various home appliances through a
centralized computer software interface. The
software system will be capable of turning
individual appliances on or off, giving the status
(on or off) of each appliance, and completing a
series of related control events, such as turning
off certain appliances and turning on others. The
system will have additional control over lamps and
other lighting devices, being able to control the
brightness of such fixtures. This document presents
the desired functionality and the known hardware and
software components of the system.

HARDWARE The system hardware will consist of a
standard Macintosh computer as the control center,
and outlet controls manufactured by the X10 company
as the interface to the home appliances. The X10
controllers are monitored by a central control box
which connects to the Macintosh through one of the
serial ports. The configuration is as follows:

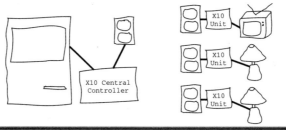

Figure 5.3 - Sample Home Control System Requirements.
This sample, on the following three pages, of a systems requirements document highlights the key elements of a requirements statement and illustrates that requirements don't have to be long or complex to be effective. Sections of the document describe

The X10 central controller communicates with the
remote unit through the standard plug outlets
already installed in the home, so no additional
hardware support should be necessary.

SOFTWARE The X10 control package comes with a series
of HyperCard XCMDs which can be used to access the
central controller. HyperCard will therefore be used
as the front end for user interaction, and the user
interface for controlling the devices will be a
HyperCard stack. While the XCMDs for interacting
with the controller exist, a number of other
constructs will be necessary for smooth user
interaction. These include:

- representations of individual devices for control,
  and a means of representing selection among them

- sequential command structures for executing series
  of related control actions (to support user
  "events" as identified in task analysis stage)

- centralized on-off control "switch" which can act
  on the currently selected device, and includes a
  dimmer to control light brightness

- construct to track information about the state of
  the various devices, such as whether it is on or
  off, and if it is a light how bright it is

key elements of the Home Control system for accessing various
home appliances remotely through a computer interface. These
key areas include system hardware (with a functional diagram),
system software and a projected schedule for development.

Each of these elements will have to be tied in with
the graphical visualization used to represent its
functionality on-screen.

SCHEDULE The following list of milestones is a rough
estimate based on understood needs of the system.

15 FEB test and incorporate existing XCMDs for
device control

1 MAR complete sequential commands for user
"events" complete control switch
with dimmer

15 MAR incorporate appropriate graphics
phase I prototype available for
user tests

10 APR update prototype based on feedback from
phase I tests phase II prototype
available for user tests

1 MAY deliver final system

Schedule system development.

An important part of the system requirements document should be a short schedule of major system milestones, including total projected time and a date at which each milestone will be delivered. Drafting a schedule early on will help you achieve important delivery dates, and accurately project the amount of time necessary to meet them. If you are working on a multi-person team, include information about each team member's responsibilities.

Steps for conducting system requirements

1. Analyze the needs of the system.

    Think about the hardware:

    *   I/O devices
    *   speed
    *   cost
    *   size
    *   color
    *   sound
    *   multi-media
    *   complexity
    *   portability
    *   integration

    Think about the software:

    *   range of tools available
    *   interconnectivity
    *   imports and exports
    *   extendibility
    *   flexibility
    *   programming language issues

2. Build small prototypes,if appropriate. Short experiments early on might help you avoid spending time later building elaborate but useless systems.

3   Draft a schedule for development, including responsibilities and deliverables

4. Work with other team members to meet all concerns. By incorporating feedback from user-focused or graphics-focused experts, you will be sure to address many aspects of the interface.

Hints/suggestions

System requirements are for you—to help you plan your system and provide a way to document your intentions. Do not feel that they must meet some strict format requirements. While you might have similar documentation required on your job, be sure to develop a derivative that answers your concerns, not just those dictated by someone else's documentation standard.

While the type of system requirements presented here are informal in nature, you might want to create a more formal format as a personal reference, so you are sure to address issues that are important to you each time you develop system requirements. Some of the "standard" sections to include might be a brief description of the system, a list of hardware and software, any constraints you are aware of ahead of time, and a tentative schedule for implementation. Of course, not every category will be important every time you draft system requirements, but having a format as a reference will help you to organize your requirements.

Use diagrams or illustrations where appropriate to clarify system features or interrelationships.

Exercise task

Draft, then write the system requirements for your supermarket guide. Your system requirements will probably be between two and five pages in length, and address the following issues:

- What is the basic purpose and function of the system? What will it do, and how will it do it?

- What hardware do you anticipate you will use for the system? Will all instances of the system (if there are more than one) have the same hardware? Is there any additional hardware that might be supported?

- On what software platform will the system run? Will you require any special programs or modules in addition to your system?

- How will you organize your own software application or system? What will be the basic structure and modules?

- Would a diagram help to illustrate how the system functions? You might want to illustrate the physical system, the hardware or software relationships, or anything else you think would clarify your requirements document.

- What is your approximate development schedule? Define the segments and how long it will take you to implement each of them. Putting dates on development schedules can be scary, but it can also help you to understand the work you must do. Reaching those milestones will help you feel as though you are accomplishing the necessary steps to get your guide built and out the door!

Method 3: Building a Backbone

Creating code that serves as the underlying structure for a developing application or system.

Sometimes short code segments built for your early on-line prototypes will not be enough to get at questionable system functionality. You will want to know if a targeted or potential software development environment meets your needs in a more general, overall sense. For these system questions, you must get at the underlying structure of the software system you are building. Designing and implementing a system driver or backbone allows you to evaluate overall system capabilities and test your software.

Create the backbone with the intention of supporting modifications in the design. Your design will undoubtedly need alternatives and changes as your goals change. The backbone should not be a rigid underlying framework that limits further design or programming work. It should be a flexible base structure that will support the emerging design all through its development. The underlying structure itself, the backbone, need not change if you have designed it to support the system development needs.

The most important element of your backbone is flexibility. It should support whatever instance data you believe will be important for you design (bitmaps, user interactions, and so forth); and you should be able to substitute data, as long as it is of the same basic type, to accommodate any further design findings. It should also be supportive of changing entire modules of the software, so that if an alternate algorithm or approach to the coding design is used, it can readily be adapted within your backbone framework. Overall, remember that you do not want the backbone to constrain any later system developments. While it is impossible to always have the foresight to know what those developments might be, keeping a flexible approach can best help you prepare for future changes.

The visible end product of your backbone need not be pretty or look much like your intended system at all. You are not writing a backbone to see what the system will look like, or even to use to show potential users to gather feedback. You and other members of the software development team are the primary customers for a backbone.

You might want to develop a backbone even when you know it won't be used as the basis of your later system. Sometimes you will develop a backbone simply to see how the whole system comes together, even if it is not on the target hardware or software platform. In this case, the backbone does not have to be in same programming language as the final system (but it helps if the languages are similar so basic constructs can be simply substituted). Of course, if you do know the targeted platform and can use it, you will probably save yourself effort in the long run if you use the same platform. But if you do not, or for some reason you cannot, you can still go a long way developing a backbone for your system.

Backbones can be particularly useful when system input or output events are known. You can put together a backbone that is event-driven and processes each incoming event with a known output event sequences. This is particularly relevant in developing event-driven Macintosh software. For instance, if you know that users can enter information into your system by clicking the mouse button, moving the mouse, or striking certain keyboard keys, then you can write a backbone that reacts to each of those actions. In doing so, you will have practiced the challenge of interpreting user input from a variety of sources.

The importance of building a backbone

A backbone can provide the basis for your future system, or at least give you some indication of how the total system will work together. It can be important for overall system development because it:

Supports underlying system structure.

A backbone is probably your first attempt at putting a whole system together. In this way, it supports your ability to analyze the entire system structure. It might cause you to evaluate the overall system in ways you previously overlooked or were unable to because of the nature of your system. Even if you do not implement a complete backbone, the effort of outlining and planning one can be a strong step toward analyzing the underlying structure of your emerging system.

Provides opportunity to practice and learn the target programming language.

Designing and implementing a backbone gives you first-hand experience with the programming language in which the backbone is developed. If you know that language is the same as the target system, writing a backbone can be an excellent way to learn or practice working in that language. You might want to consider writing a backbone or segments of one on alternate platforms to help you evaluate programming languages or environments, if your target platform is not known. This way, you can use a real task—creating the basis for your system—as an evaluation of potential platforms.

Practices ability to interpret input and output (I/O) options.

When input and output alternatives are known, developing a backbone gives you the opportunity to test your ability to support potential interactions. Even if all I/O options are not known, you might use the backbone to evaluate the alternatives, or to test your system's ability to adequately support potential options.

Provides potential to learn about the platform.

Not only will developing a backbone help you to learn about the language in which it is written, it can teach you about the hardware platform, as well. Even if the hardware platform on which you are currently working is not the same as your target platform, you can begin grappling with issues that are common to both environments, such as: screen size and image resolution constraints, system memory and data object size requirements, operating speed or feedback constraints. When you do eventually move to your target platform, you will be better prepared to address these hardware-dependency issues.

Saves time later.

One very good reason to build a backbone for your system is that it very likely will save you development time down the road. This is particularly true if you are able to use your backbone as the underlying code for your final system. However, even if you don't end up using the backbone itself, developing it will serve as a trial run. By showing you the parameters that will be important later on, it can be a valuable time saver in the development process.

Steps for building a backbone

1. Identify the basic functionality you will be building.

2. Identify input and output routines (such as interpreting mouse events or drawing bitmaps to a screen).

3. Write and run a simple driver. Practice software building activities that will be used in system development, such as compiling, linking, and running.

4. Structure your routines and file organization (if appropriate).

5. Implement your basic routines.

6. Use sample data to try out your routines. Better yet, if you have representative data (such as scanned bitmaps from earlier prototypes), use that.

Hints/suggestions

- Consider drivers you built previously, either for prototyping purposes or as part of another application or system. Reuse anything you can.

- Write pseudo code first. As with any other programming exercise, pseudo code will help you to organize your thoughts and provide a structure for when you actually begin coding. Pseudo code can also serve as your comments in the coded version.

- Don't worry about the front end of the system. Running a backbone might mean lots of empty screens and <<[something] will go here>> notices in place of the user interface. While your backbone should support whatever user interface you eventually design based on user and system needs, in its initial stages, it is not intended to represent your final system.

- Use your backbone to test the appropriateness of the programming language or environment for your task. If this is a familiar environment, does it have the necessary constructs as you remember them? If it is a new environment, will it be able to support the functionality you will need? Write more than one backbone in alternate environments to compare them, if necessary.

Exercise task

Design and write a backbone for your supermarket guide. Use this opportunity to identify the programming environment you will use for your guide, and to try different aspects of the programming environments that are available to you. Consider these issues:

- Does the programming environment you have chosen meet your needs? What is particularly good or bad about it? Might other environments be more appropriate?

- Is the backbone extensible? Can you easily plug in code segments or routines at a later time? Will you easily be able to incorporate code segments that others write in the future?

- Have you made your data interpretation adaptable so that alternate bitmaps, sounds, or other data types can be changed readily?

- Is your backbone portable to other hardware platforms, if necessary? Or, if your guide will run on more than one hardware platform, have you designed the code to adapt to all platforms with minimal modifications?

- What are the implementation procedures, such as compiling, linking, binding, and executing your code? How might this affect your development process?

Method 4: The Power of Clip Art

Collecting computer-based illustrations, drawings, photographs, or other images that are incorporated in on-line applications.

Visual elements are a critical part of graphical user interfaces. While visual presentation can be important in off-line prototyping as well, the ultimate success of the graphical component of a software system is often tied to the final graphics presented on the screen. As a result, on-line artwork can be critical for software development. Final graphics need not be determined early on in the design process, but the earlier the graphic needs are addressed, the more likely they will be adequately supported in the final system. Clip art, or computer-based visuals that can be incorporated in on-line applications, are an important part of on-line development.

Visual integrity or communication is often a critical factor in the legibility or success of a user interface, but developers typically don't want to take the time early on to create custom visuals. If you are attempting to judge feasibility of an overall interactive strategy, or qualify functionality of the system, then it seems silly to spend time creating detailed graphics that might be omitted in a later version of the system. Still, you will want quality visuals to communicate your intentions in a way that is as true to the final system as possible. Using clip art can solve your short-term problems and help you understand important long-term issues about the visual aspects of your final system.

Think of clip art as a collection of on-line images that you gather over time—your reference library of visual imagery. You will turn to it to find an image to represent a certain function, or for background art to set an overall mood. You might use imagery from your clip art collection directly, or change details to best meet your needs at the time. You will find with practice that you can cut and paste parts of your images together to create precisely the image you need for a particular feature. Changing simple details, like the font or style of text that is included as part of the image, or the thickness or color of a line, can make the difference in your ability to communicate the message you want.

Sources of clip art

There are numerous sources of clip art. You can:

- Purchase it from third party vendors.

- Download it from public access bulletin boards or databases.

- Draw it on the computer using a draw or paint application.

- Create it off-line and scan or trace it electronically to convert it to an on-line format.

- Create a composite of off-line and on-line images—for example, an off-line design that is scanned in, then manipulated using on-line tools.

Today's Macintosh draw and paint applications offer a wide range of excellent tools for creating and altering visual designs. Clip art can be created by a single person or by multiple designers over time. It doesn't really matter where the clip art comes from or how it was created. It's more important that you continually add to your collection of images so that the more designs you do, the more options you have for finding the perfect visual.

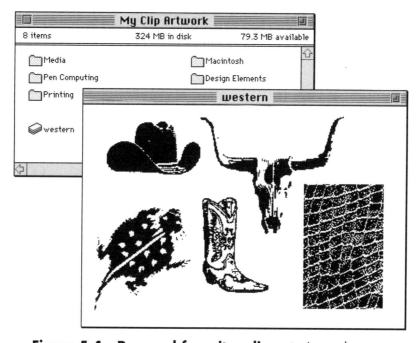

Figure 5.4 - Personal favorites clip art. A good way to ensure you always have access to a range of clip art is to keep and build your own library of clip art. As you come across images or libraries that you like, make a copy on your local machine. You will probably have preferences for certain image styles or need for certain application area illustrations, and keeping your own libraries can help you keep track of these. This may seem like trivial information, but keeping a centralized version of your own personal clip art favorites can save you significant time at design time when you are looking for just the right image.

Storing clip art

If you will store your clip art on-line, spend time planning how to organize it. Clip art can be storage consuming: individual images, particularly 8-bit (or more) color images, can quickly consume all the storage space available on your hard disk. I am not advocating that you gather many large images and plant them on your hard disk for eternity. However, you might want to consider investing in a storage strategy (such as a removable hard disk unit) that will enable you to keep your images available for quick access.

With time and experience, you will determine how best to store these images. Individual files of each image in a particular application format (such as Adobe's Photoshop or Fractal's Painter) will probably be the most storage consuming option, but will allow you the most flexible access to the image. Storing images in subsequent cards of a HyperCard stack might limit your ability to access original image features, but might be an efficient way to store 2-bit bitmap-based images. You might want to use some combination of storage strategies to keep the different types of art that you collect.

A major advantage of using the Macintosh as your development platform is that images can be stored easily in a common format (PICT or TIFF, for example). These formats support imagery that can be readily imported and exported to and from a variety of applications. This means that as long as you store your images in one of these common file formats, you will be able to access it from any number of applications that support that image format. Again, storing all your images as individual files will require lots of storage space, but for certain images this might prove beneficial.

One strategy you can use that might help is to store more than one image in a single file of a paint application, particularly if all the images fit on a single page or screen. These types of applications often store all the color information for the entire page, even if the image occupies only a small area of that page.

Figure 5.5 - HyperCard clip art. A number of clip art resources are available to the user interface designer for visually representing interface elements. HyperCard comes with a variety of clip art images, as shown here in the Art Bits stack.

Using clip art in prototyping

Clip art is especially useful when developing prototypes; you can simply flip through your library of images to pull in one that meets your needs. Clip art in prototyping is particularly helpful if it can be used efficiently as a place holder for the later final images. Take steps in your on-line design development to see that image substitution is a simple process, if this will be part of your development strategy.

When you know that you will substitute your clip art for original art later, you have a wide range of possibilities for temporary images, such as scanning in photographs or even using original art from other applications. You won't use such images in your final system (either for legal or artistic reasons), but you can save time now by using them as a temporary image. This is particularly true when the details and specifications for the final artwork are likely to change significantly as your system emerges.

Depending on the clip art you have available and your project, you might be able to use the clip art from your prototypes in your final software. But remember, this is not the intention of clip art, nor is it the norm for how it is used.

The importance of clip art

Clip art can be useful in the on-line development stages for a number of reasons. It is worth investing some time developing a clip art library, adding to it, and refining it. The time you spend will pay off repeatedly. Some of the ways clip art can help you in your design process are that it:

Saves you time because you will have less need to create custom imagery.

Time devoted to gathering images when you have free time to do so can save you significant time later when you are under schedule pressures to complete software projects. While it might seem difficult to pull together clip art images when you can't be sure exactly what type of imagery you will need, you will learn with experience the types of images that will be most appropriate for the types of projects on which you typically work.

Allows you to attend to visual design in early prototyping stages.

Because the earlier stages of development are typically devoted to getting at general functionality or overall direction rather than individual details, and because exact visual representation of imagery can be thought of as specific detail, the visual elements of your design are often overlooked in earlier phases. With clip art you can still attend to the visual elements of your design without having to commit to exact images. You might, of course, need to spend time later refining your visuals, but that will come at a design stage when you are ready to make visual detail decisions.

Gives you ideas for what you might really want.

Sometimes you will need a visual for your design but not know exactly what you want in your image. This can be true even if you are a skilled visual designer with the role of providing the visual identity of a software project. Looking through your clip art library and trying various options can give you ideas for what you might want in your later imagery. At the very least, it might point out what you don't want to use, and help narrow your search for the appropriate visuals.

Requires minimal effort to gather and maintain a clip art library.

You can develop a useful and robust clip art library with minimal effort, particularly if you have a simple strategy in place. Such a strategy might be always storing interesting images on a certain removable hard disk cartridge. The marginal amount of time you spend can pay off significantly later.

Helps you develop a personal style that "trademarks" your prototypes or later work.

Developing your own clip art library can help you to institute and cultivate an individual image style that can "trademark" your software projects. (This might or might not be important to you, depending on the nature of your work.) As you gather and alter images in your clip art collection, your images can evolve into visuals that are indicative of your personality.

Steps for collecting and using clip art

1. Look at the images available in the application software you already have.

2. Make a dedicated folder on your machine for gathering all clip art, and put whatever you find in there. When you come across useful imagery, simply put a copy in this folder.

3. Consider hard copy images, as well. Look through old maga-
    zines or drawings. If you have time, go "shopping" at a library
    or book store to see what types of illustrations are available
    to you.

4. Scan in interesting textures and patterns from objects you
    find, such as leather or wood grain. These might be useful to
    give background character to your prototypes, and can be place
    holders for further designs.

Hints/suggestions

*   Be aware of potential copyright issues with the images you
    gather. You are free to use any image for intermediate proto-
    types, and using pre-existing images will save you time and
    effort. However, if you plan to incorporate some of these
    images in software that you will sell for a profit, you might
    be limited in the imagery you can use.

*   Obtain and use on-line software tools that can help you
    quickly and easily grab parts of images and take them from
    one application to another. Such tools exist on the Macin-
    tosh.

Exercise task

Begin gathering clip art that you think might be useful in your supermarket
guide. Consider the functionality you are planning to include, then consider
what types of imagery would be useful for your system. Some things to think
about:

*   Include images from on-line clip art sources, and scan in
    images from books, magazines, illustrations, and drawings.

*   Practice manipulating the scanned images and tailoring them
    to your needs.

- Use visuals from materials you gathered during your early
  user study phase.

- If you are able to, create custom imagery you think might be
  useful. A pen-based tablet with one of today's advanced paint
  programs (such as Fractal's Painter) can provide a range of creative opportunities for making impressive and appropriate
  visuals.

Method 5: On-line Flipbooks

**A prototype on the computer that illustrates system func-
tionality by linking together, screen by screen, the system
images with the system interaction.**

Flipbooks are useful in off-line prototyping because they link together the
representation of various user interface elements with the behavior that
defines system interaction. (See the Flipbooks section in Chapter 4.) Extending the notion of flipbooks to on-line representations can have similar benefits for your computer-based designs. On-line flipbooks link the visual elements of your system (that is, individual screens or subsets of screens) with
user interaction. You can begin to piece together the workings of the final
software system. They take the off-line flipbooks a step further by presenting the interaction on the computer, and thereby approximating much more
closely the working of the target system.

On-line flipbooks help you to get at concrete details that you might have
overlooked when developing an off-line flipbook, but still save you the trouble of completely building the real system before you're ready. You can use
on-line flipbooks to link together whatever parts of your system you happen
to have implemented, or to structure the segments of your system that you
want to target for design or usability testing purposes. Building partial systems with on-line flipbooks will help you further your design process with-

out having to commit to a certain implementation or without having to attend to all the parts of your system.

While you can build an on-line flipbook in whatever software development environment you plan to use for your final software, you might choose instead to use a prototyping environment that readily lends itself to the screen-to-screen movement of a flipbook. On the Macintosh, tools like HyperCard provide an excellent platform for building flipbooks.

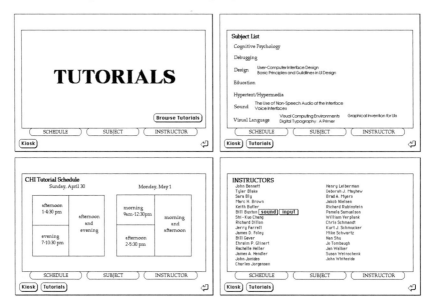

Figure 5.6 - On-line flipbooks for CHI'89 tutorials. The screens of an elementary Hypercard stack are shown here. They were used as part of an on-line prototype to explore navigation and functionality for part of the CHI'89 InfoBooth Kiosks, developed by Apple Computer's ATG Human Interface Group for the SIGCHI conference in 1989. While the design of the final kiosk was significantly different than that shown here, this early on-line flipbook helped to try out and test the interactivity of this section of the system.

Flipbooks and HyperCard

HyperCard's stack model supports a logical screen-by-screen design, and its goto linking structure allows you to easily link user actions to screens. Hyper-Card is particularly good for on-line flipbooks when the basic method of inter-action is user mouse clicks. It does not work as well when the interface requires that user interaction to be synched with real-time activities, such as sound or video technologies. Still, for the purpose of testing your on-line concepts with an on-line flipbook, it might be worth designing an abstracted version of your system and linking screens together with HyperCard. The advantage here is that you can quickly pull together some of the basic con-cepts of your system without investing time and energy in actually getting the system to work, especially at early design stages when the design proba-bly still has much evolution to go through.

Using on-line flipbooks

On-line flipbooks serve as excellent platforms for user studies, or to com-municate design ideas to other team members. Just like off-line flipbooks, they allow you to piece together the visual and interactive elements of your system. Having an on-line representation of even part of your system to include in user studies can provide you with valuable feedback on how users respond to the basic components of your system.

Sometimes it is appropriate to do an on-line flipbook instead of an off-line flipbook, depending on your available time and other constraints imposed by your particular system. Or, you can do the on-line flipbook as a later step in the development process, after an off-line flipbook has been designed and used. You might be able to reuse some of the concepts in your off-line flip-book in your on-line version, either by converting the images and interac-tions to an on-line representation, or by directly scanning in some of the visu-als from the off-line design.

You might want to develop a custom on-line structure to support your flip-book. If you find yourself using the same software development environment again and again, invest the time to design the structure that supports on-line flipbooks. You might want to use a custom backbone to structure the flipbook. Your development strategy will depend on the nature of the software environment in which you build the backbone and on the type of software you are designing.

The importance of on-line flipbooks

The advantages of using on-line flipbooks are similar to advantages of off-line flipbooks—they help you to piece together elements of the system, link interaction to visuals, and save you development time. Some specific advantages of on-line flipbooks are that they:

Allow you to address more system details.

On-line flipbooks support more specific system details than their off-line counterparts because they are computer-based. They require you to address issues like the actual size of the screens or images, the exact user interactions, and real response times in changing imagery or reacting to user input. You can tailor them to address only the details of a particular design instance, rather than every detail of the full system.

Help in user studies.

On-line flipbooks are particularly useful in user studies to obtain feedback on the aspects of your system that your flipbook showcases. They allow you to get at issues through your user studies that off-line flipbooks might not be able to support, since they more directly reflect details of the final system. Some such issues might include user reactions to actual response times, more representative visuals, or a particular input device.

Link contributions from multiple team members.

On-line formats might lend themselves more readily to a group development effort, particularly if the platform for the flipbook is readily available to everyone and supports merging of the different screens or files. (HyperCard, for instance, supports copying cards from one stack to another. While it is not the ideal group development environment, if the combined flipbook goal is known from the start of the design, it can be achieved with relative ease in HyperCard.) Combining efforts in an on-line flipbook will often create a more consistent and continuous-looking prototype, whereas a combined off-line effort often shows the different styles of its contributors.

Introduce some platform issues.

The process of designing and building an on-line flipbook will introduce you to both hardware and software issues for the particular platform you are using. Even if the flipbook is only a skeletal or partial representation of your final system, it will point out platform dependencies you can not address as directly in your off-line prototypes.

Provide a good start for later system development.

By introducing the platform dependencies of your system, an on-line flipbook is often an excellent start to your computer-based development—particularly when time or system constraints prevent you from completing other earlier on-line prototypes. On-line flipbooks can be a great way to start translating your designs onto the computer.

Steps for building on-line flipbooks

1. Decide on your hardware and software platforms. If practical, use the platforms for the target system. If not, consider using a development tool that readily lends itself to flipbook creation, such as HyperCard.

2. Identify the features and functions of your system.

3. Consider the purpose of your on-line flipbook. If you will use it in user studies, you will have different concerns than if you are developing it as a team design effort.

4. Create the screen images for your flipbook. They will probably be the screens for the final system, though not necessarily.

5. Organize the images in an appropriate order.

6. Determine which interactions will link which screens. Incorporate those interactions in your prototype.

7. Try out the flipbook to see if it works as you anticipated. You might have to make adjustments to account for speed or other details.

8. If you will use the flipbook for user studies, check to see that interactions necessary to the flipbook but that will not be part of the final system do not mislead the user. You might have to trap for certain user interactions to maintain an accurate representation of the target system.

Hints/suggestions

• While you will address more details here than in your off-line flipbooks, try not to get bogged down in irrelevant details. You can use placeholder graphics, if necessary. On-line flipbooks are still an intermediate prototype, so don't spend unnecessary time developing them.

• Incorporate clip art, even if only as place holders, so that you can link the interaction to the prototype. You can always go back and replace the visuals later.

• On-line flipbooks are excellent for demonstrations and user studies. With practice, you can make your on-line flipbooks look like your target system, and your audience will assume they are using the real working version.

• Use on-line flipbook development as an opportunity to evaluate potential hardware and software platforms. Try out the features of that platform, and see how appropriate they are for the purposes of your system.

Exercise task

Build an on-line flipbook for your supermarket guide. If you can, plan to use it for a user study or usability evaluation. (You might save it for some of the testing exercises in Chapter 7.) Consider the following items:

- How much of the system functionality will you represent?

- What platform will you use? Try to use the platform of your target system. (If you cannot do so, consider an alternative such as a platform that will support any user studies you intend to do).

- What type of images will you incorporate? First consider those readily available to you; create custom imagery, if necessary.

- Will you include any other "special" elements of your system? For instance, if you plan to use sound or video in your guide, include at least a few of these elements. This helps with implementation details and provides a more realistic representation with which to test your system.

Chapter 6

Prototyping

What is Prototyping?

I use the term prototyping to refer to all design-oriented efforts of software development. It is, in essence, all that I have been talking about in the preceding chapters. Prototypes model some aspect of the system; for user interface design, prototypes typically present some interactive element of the system. The term prototyping often refers specifically to software designs—prototypes are thought to be versions of the software developed before the final software design is executed. However, in its most loose sense, a prototype can be anything that serves a design purpose in designing and building a software application or system. While the most common instances of prototypes might be in software, prototypes can be developed off-line as well, using methodologies such as those presented in Chapter 4. A prototype is qualified by the purpose it serves, not by the form it takes.

Prototyping is the process of designing something, off- or on-line, that demonstrates some feature or interactive element of your intended system. Using the prototype, you can evaluate that design, incorporate any changes in your

155

next prototype, and eventually refine the design for your final software application or system. The evaluation process typically involves potential users to offer feedback on the working of the system, although not all stages of prototyping need to involve user input.

Other terms used to describe this general process include rapid prototyping and iterative design. The rapid in rapid prototyping refers to the speed with which you generate these designs, typically because the robustness or working quality of the designs are less important at this stage, allowing you to focus on the design itself. Iterative design refers to the cyclical nature of the prototyping design process (and is further discussed in Chapter 8). In user interface design, prototyping is typically a repeated process, with each iteration moving you closer to the final system design.

The unifying characteristic of all prototypes is that they serve as an aid in the design process. They are not intended to be a final deliverable, and can (and should!) be thought of as expendable. This is not to say that you will automatically trash everything you build as a prototype, or that you will never incorporate your prototyping work in your target system. However, you should not necessitate using a prototype for your actual software. If the prototype indicates something doesn't quite work, then you should be ready to dispense with it and continue prototyping until you find something that does. A prototype is simply an early or intermediate design that gets at some points of the target system.

Which functions or interactive elements a user interface prototype addresses will depend on its purpose, when it is developed in relation to other system milestones, and the other prototypes that have preceded it or are planned to follow it. A prototype is used to try out or test one or more design principles, to allow you to explore user interface functionality, and possibly present that functionality in a format that can be used to obtain feedback from potential users. In developing a prototype, you should not worry about whether the implementation is as it will be on your target delivery system, or that the concerns of that system are necessarily addressed. Instead, you should focus on communicating the design aspect for which the prototype was built. Once that user interface design element is working, you can determine if you will incorporate it in your target system.

Most of this chapter presents a general design approach to prototyping, referring to prototyping as a whole, giving an overview of its role. The methods sections refer specifically to software prototyping tools, providing information on what is available. Software prototyping tools allow you to translate many of the beneficial elements of user interface design to your on-line versions. Since the techniques and benefits of other prototyping approaches are presented in earlier chapters, they are not reiterated here.

How to approach prototyping

Prototyping on- or off-line can be in many formats and for many purposes, as is evident by the range of techniques already presented. Some projects will lead you to apply many of the methodologies; other projects will require only one or two methodologies. Deciding which prototyping techniques to apply is an integral part of your design process, and is discussed in the preceding chapters and summarized below. There are many different ways to design, build, and test your software application or system. However, only you can be the judge of what will work best for your needs. The process can be well directed if you understand how to correctly apply judgment criteria and evaluate your needs.

In many ways, prototyping is a state of mind. You must:

- Recognize that prototyping is necessary for a robust and successful design.

- Plan carefully and choose wisely from among the many prototyping techniques you can apply to your design.

- Build into your schedule and budget the time and resources necessary for adequate prototyping.

- Perform the prototyping itself. You might need to revise your plan or your prototypes, depending on your results.

- Recognize that iterative prototyping is truly the best way to incorporate the concerns of your users in your software design—which is, after all, the purpose of user interface design

The Advantages of Prototyping

Acknowledging the value of prototyping and including it in your software development process is probably the most important thing you can do to enhance the way you design your software and its user interface. Prototyping user interface designs can be advantageous because it:

Can be done using whatever tools you have or prefer.

The general process of prototyping does not require any particular materials or tools. You can build prototypes with whatever is available to you and with whatever makes the most sense at the time of development. Certainly the tools and materials you use will make some difference in the nature and quality of your prototypes, but for general purposes you can build many aspects of your design with tools and materials you already have around.

Can take as little or as much time as you have.

Prototyping does not assume any given amount of time, or necessitate any particular minimal time to get worthwhile results. Clearly the more time you have to devote to prototyping, the more user interface details you will be able to address and the more robust your system will be. Still, even if you have only a few days or hours, spending some time mocking up elements of your design and evaluating how they meet the users' needs can be critical in designing your software system.

Involves users in the design process to best meet their needs.

Prototypes can be incorporated readily into user studies or usability tests; showing prototypes to potential users can, in fact, be the most valuable aspect of developing them. User feedback can save you hours, days, or weeks of development time spent on the mechanics of a system feature, only to find that it is unnecessary in your design. When you prototype just the interactive feature, without worrying about how it will be implemented, you will be surprised at how quickly you can put a prototype together. Even the most sparse of prototypes can be shown to users to obtain feedback, and only towards the end of your design cycle will you typically need to worry about making the prototype closely mimic the features of your actual system. Prototyping enables you to design systems that best meet user needs because you can involve users through interaction with your prototypes.

Allows developers to focus on what they want to.

Because you can build a prototype that exemplifies only the elements of your system in which you are interested, you can save yourself the time of developing a full-blown system. Too often software developers will wait "until the system is working" to try out anything, either for design purposes or to use as part of a usability study. Proper prototyping recognizes the value of using a partial system to get at the initial design elements, without having to wait for a whole system to be built. Developers can focus on the aspects of their designs they think are most important; once those elements are satisfactory, they can go on to develop the whole system.

Supports integrating known or desired features.

It is up to you how much of your target application or system you will include in any prototype you develop. You can include as much as you know about the system, or as little as you want to, depending on what you aim to accomplish with the prototype. The ability to integrate whatever features you feel appropriate—rather than every feature that exists or must exist for the system to be functional—is possible because of the flexible nature of prototyping.

Supports an incremental, iterative design process.

Since prototyping promotes the inclusion of only the features you want to test at any particular time, it clearly supports a cyclical, incremental approach to software development. Even if you can support only one round of prototyping, you are making a commitment to an iterative design process. Iteration plays a key role in robust and user-sensitive software designs.

Guides the building of better systems.

Ultimately, using prototypes will almost always result in a better designed, better built system. You will be able to address basic structure and behavioral concerns of your user interface without the influences of the actual software design, allowing you to focus on the design itself rather than making the software work. Believing in the importance of prototyping and making it work in your design process will truly guide you to develop better software applications and systems.

How to Select, Design, and Perform Prototyping Techniques

The earlier techniques chapters (Chapters 3, 4, and 5) provide information about what the different prototyping techniques can achieve and why you might use them. They do not, however, offer much guidance as to whether you should perform some of each of the different types of techniques, or focus your effort on one particular type of prototyping. While there is no specific formula for determining how much time to devote to user studies, off-line prototypes, and on-line prototypes, there are a number of factors you can consider that will help you make these decisions for your design. The following factors, together with the criteria given for each of these three types of techniques presented in the earlier chapters, should guide you in your decision on which methods make the most sense for you.

Overall schedule

As with all types of techniques, you are probably most directed by any time constraints on your project. If you know you have to deliver your final soft-

ware on a certain date, then you can work backward from that date to determine time limits on the particular aspects of prototyping you want to achieve.
Time alone will not help you identify which techniques to use, nor whether
to develop on-line or off-line prototypes. However, knowing your time limitations will help you evaluate other factors.

As noted in earlier chapters, you will probably want to spend approximately
one-third of your time in early studies and the pre-design stages, one-third of
your time building your system, and one-third of your time testing and iterating the design. This is not a universal formula, and it does not mean that
you should spend one-third of your time on all three of the earlier design
methods. If you look at software prototyping as part of building your target
system, then you might be able to plan for some of your software prototyping as part of the system design time. Likewise, if you plan to invest time in
user studies involving your prototypes, then you probably will not need a full
third of your time for testing and iteration at the end of the process since
much of that will happen throughout.

Available resources

Sometimes you will know which prototypes make the most sense to use
based on the resources you have available. Consider the skills and experience
of the people on your design team, the materials and tools that are available
to you (including hardware and software for on-line work), and the facilities
in which you can create and present any prototypes. Often it will make good
sense to take advantage of what is readily available to you first, before you
invest additional time or money in alternatives.

While you don't want to limit yourself to certain prototypes simply because
you can do them, if you aren't sure which prototypes will be most appropriate, then first build those that make the most sense from a resource perspective. You can always build additional prototypes if the first round does
not meet your design needs.

Your final software

Sometimes you will be able to decide about which prototypes to build from analyzing the characteristics of your target system. If you do not yet know anything about your target system, then you cannot take advantage of this. However, most of the time some decisions have been made about the target system, be they specifics about cost, size, hardware or software.

Choose a prototyping tool or environment based on what you know about the target system. You might choose a specific software development package because it runs on your target hardware. Or you might use a tool that supports sound and video if you know you will incorporate these into your final system. Mapping from your target system to your prototyping development system can help you to understand what types of software prototypes (or even off-line prototypes or studies) make the most sense for your designs.

The nature of what you are developing

Analyze more closely the design you are developing or the overall software. This will help you get a feel for how loose you want to keep your prototypes. If the concepts you are presenting are relatively new to your target user population, then you will probably want to start with studies to get information for your design and then build low-overhead off-line designs to get feedback on the overarching concepts. If, however, you are designing a piece that is only incrementally different than something with which your users are quite familiar, then you can probably forego some of the earlier stages of design and work with software prototypes right away.

You are free to use whatever design techniques make the most sense for your designs. If you happen to have a working version of the software for which you are designing a revision or replacement, then you might want to start with a usability study, since your users are familiar with the larger concepts already. You can use information from such research to help you design your alternative software.

Access to users

Before you begin, think about how you might involve users in your proto-typing work.

- Will you plan many studies that require user involvement?

- Will you use the same people in each of the studies, or get "fresh" users for each revision?

- Do you have some users ready and waiting, or will you have to recruit participants for your studies?

- Are your participants cooperative and supportive, or will you need to think about influencing them to help you?

- Will you need to compensate your participants in any way?

Thinking about all of these details up front will help give you a better under-standing of the scope of user involvement for this project, and what kinds of time and cost commitments you will have to make to support them.

How you will use the prototypes

Think about why you are building the prototypes at all, and who the audi-ence is for them. If the prototypes are simply for design purposes—to share among members of your design team or for your own review—then they prob-ably need not be too polished or complete. If, however, the prototypes are for usability studies or tests, they will need to be more thoroughly thought out and robust. Similarly, if you plan to use them to document your design process or to communicate the design progress to either your management or clients, then you will probably want them to be more permanent in nature. Being clear about the intent of your designs might help influence you in choosing the types of prototypes to build.

Past experience

Look at the prototypes you built before. Try to remember why they did or did not work well. See if the same reasoning applies to your current design project. If storyboarding worked well for you in the past, it will probably be worth your while to storyboard again. Likewise, if you haven't had much success with on-line flipbooks, you will probably want to stay away from them. Look also at prototypes that your colleagues (and possibly even your competitors) have designed, and consider if those kinds of pieces would work for you in your current situation. Your own experiences can tell you a lot about why certain types of prototypes might be appropriate for your current design.

Method 1: Planning and Scheduling

Allocation of time and resources to the user-centered prototyping approach of software design and understanding the effects on the overall design process.

Talking about planning and scheduling might seem unnecessary, but since it is an integral part of the prototyping process, and since few software engineers I know devote adequate time to thinking about their designs before building them, I am including this section as a guide. All too often, planning for prototypes—as well as for the actual system software—is overlooked or given inadequate time. In order for prototyping to truly help you with your design process, it must be planned for and scheduled into the overall development process.

Before you can adequately plan your user interface design prototyping, you must understand the array of options available to you, and you need to have a sense about which ones make the most sense for your particular design. That's why the chapters detailing specific prototyping methods precedes this section on planning and scheduling. Practicing the methods and gaining familiarity with the cost and benefit tradeoffs among them will help you become more adept at planning overall system development. By knowing something about each, or even some, of the techniques, you will have a head start on choosing the work that will make the most sense for your design and in planning your development process.

The excuse I hear most often for why people do not plan or develop a realistic prototyping schedule is that they did not have enough time to make it worthwhile. Even if the time you have to devote to prototyping and development is extremely short, whether it is limited to a week or even a day, planning ahead will pay off tremendously in the long run. Making the best use of that time, however, requires forethought about which processes can yield results that you can reasonably incorporate in your designs. Without planning in advance, you risk wasting what little prototyping time you have.

Effective planning and scheduling does not mean developing an elaborate process or following an unrealistic development cycle. At its most basic, planning and scheduling involves these three activities:

1. Thinking about which of the prototyping procedures make the most sense for your design. Consider which methods can most easily be implemented and will be most beneficial for your particular design.

2. Writing the procedures down as a plan, using the documentation format with which you are most comfortable. Include basic time frames and deliverables, as well as indicating who will carry out the prototyping. Work backward from any known deadlines or incorporate any known constraints. Bring attention to the importance of prototyping so that you are sure to get support for conducting it.

3. Showing the plan to others, perhaps those on your design team or your management, to gather feedback as to whether or not it makes sense. Try to gather unbiased feedback as to whether or not your approach will work.

```
                    Development Plan
                     Home Library

Project Dates:  March 1 - June 30, 1992

User Observation of library visitors.
        Date of Completion:  March 15, 1992
        Staff:  Susan Richards
        Critical Resources:  Video camera

Task Analysis of users conducting and organizing
research.
        Date of Completion:  March 31, 1992
        Staff:  Susan Richards

Scenarios and storyboards for Home Library.
        Date of Completion:  April 10, 1992
        Staff:  Bryan Bower

Studies of users with early prototypes of Home
Library.
        Date of Completion:  April 25, 1992
        Staff:  Susan Richards
        Critical Resources:  Video camera

Hypercard prototypes of Home Library system.
        Date of Completion:  May 31, 1992
        Staff:  Bryan Bower
        Critical Resources:  Macintosh Powerbook 140

Usability tests of prototypes.
        Date of Completion:  June 15, 1992
        Staff:  Susan Richards
        Critical Resources:  Video camera, Macintosh
        Powerbook 140
```

Figure 6.1 - Plan and schedule for home library prototype. A sample prototyping plan for a home library reference system is presented here. A milestone for each stage of development is listed, along with expected completion dates, design team member(s) responsible and projected resource needs.

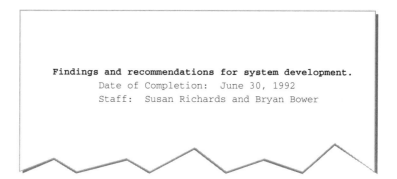

The importance of planning and scheduling

Planning and scheduling are valuable activities because they:

Save time in the long run.

Thinking about what prototypes you might build and what makes the most sense for your design will not only give you a better understanding of your work, it will help you better understand the design process for this project and for every project you will undertake in the future. The efficiency and relevance of the work you do toward your final software will more than make up for the time you spend planning it.

Help you to identify work practices that make the most sense for your design.

Making a plan and a schedule really will help you to identify the process that will be best for your prototyping and software design. Writing your ideas down on paper will give you perspective on your thoughts, and help you to see details that you might have overlooked when thinking about or even verbalizing your intentions. You will realize that certain processes are not feasible in the time frame you have, or that the product of certain prototyping techniques might not be valuable for your effort. Planning and scheduling can help you to better understand the prototyping processes as they apply to your project.

Help you to think about how to best use resources.

When you write down the prototyping processes you plan to tackle and the people and materials you plan to apply to each prototype, you will get a better overall picture of who will be doing what on this project. Just thinking about the techniques and prototypes sometimes does not help you to see that you were over-committing one design team member and not taking advantage of another. Likewise, you might assume that you are capable of achieving more than is actually feasible given your time or budget constraints. When you write down a plan that lists each projected prototype and milestone along with who and what it will take to achieve it, you leave nothing to question. You can best allocate your available resources, as well as realize where additional resources will be necessary.

Keep you in touch with the overall development.

Thinking about and executing your plan will help you keep track of your entire prototyping process. If you keep up with your plan, particularly if it is for a long period of time, and update it according to changes you make, you will have a record of what you achieved. This can be useful in reviewing or documenting your current process, as well as helping you the next time you plan a prototyping effort. Even if you do not update the plan as your work progresses, having a record of what you originally intended can be extremely useful for tracking your efforts.

Help to ensure that prototyping really happens.

Putting together a plan and then using it to conduct and track your work might be a disciplinary action that actually ensures that prototyping happens when it otherwise would not. Certainly, if you don't think about what you will do, then chances are it will not happen. If you don't plan for a certain number of prototypes by certain dates, then the tendency will be to allow preliminary procedures to drag out longer than anticipated. This is not to say that making a plan will guarantee a successful prototyping and design effort, but it is a step in the right direction and will rarely deter you from success.

Steps for planning and scheduling

1. Identify a final delivery date for the project. If a formal one doesn't exist, create one.

2. Work backward from that date, estimating how much time you will spend in research, off-line prototyping, on-line prototyping, and actual system development.

3. Determine milestones for each phase. Identify a delivery date for each milestone.

4. Identify resources for each milestone, such as who will work on that milestone and any equipment needed.

5. Share your plan with colleagues. Obtain consensus from those who will be working on the plan, those who expect the final software delivery, and anyone else appropriate in your circumstances.

Hints/suggestions

- While each project will require a slightly different approach, a good rule of thumb is to spend about half of the time in design (research, off-line prototyping and on-line prototyping) and the other half building the actual system. If this seems like too much time in design, remember that if it is done correctly, prototyping should actually reduce system development time. Knowing this, you might even consider spending more than half your overall time on prototyping.

- Realize that plans might change and schedules slip. Still, try to be as accurate as possible at the onset. If the situation changes, update your plan.

- Use the planning phase to make a first guess at which of the methods will be appropriate for your project. Knowing which types of design techniques you will use will probably prove valuable in estimating time to be spent. Likewise, if you know the time you want to spend, that might help you define the tasks to which you will apply the techniques.

Exercise task

If you have already completed many of the prototyping steps in earlier exercises, it might seem somewhat after the fact at this point to plan a schedule for the remainder of your prototyping efforts. Concentrate on planning how to convert your prototype designs to your target software system. (You might need to read the following method sections before you can complete this exercise.) While preparing for this exercise task, think about:

- What is your overall time frame?

- How much of that time will you need to devote to actual system development and how much will you have available for prototyping?

- What are the resources available to you? How can you best match your skills to the methods?

- What kinds of prototyping techniques will work best for you? Of those that will work well, how many will you have time to apply?

Method 2: Selecting the Right Tools

Analyzing your development needs and identifying tools with which you can build your prototypes and the system.

The preceding chapters focus on the design aspects of software development, presenting various prototyping methodologies and ways to design your software before you actually build it. The focus on design techniques has been to emphasize that much can be done to facilitate the design and implementation process, not to trivialize the importance of sound software implementation. The process of making the software work—of building an actual software application or system—is far from trivial. It is clearly critical to the effectiveness of the final system. Using the right tools, both in the early design and prototyping phases and in the actual implementation, can make a tremendous difference in the efficiency and success of your software development process.

In this section, the term tool (software development tools) applies to any aid in the design process, be it a physical implement used in off-line prototypes or a software environment used to develop prototypes or your final software. Selecting which tools to use for a particular project can be critical to the success of your software. Sometimes the choice of tools to use will be obvious, or you will have experience which leads you to select one tool over another. However, at some point in your software development career, whether it is the very first time you prototype or later when your familiar tools no longer meet your needs, you will use some criteria to help you choose which tools to use for particular tasks.

Keep in mind that some tools might serve more than one purpose, or that different tools might offer similar benefits. Likewise, tools that seem quite similar might offer significantly different benefits at different costs. In evaluating which tools are right for your design purposes, you will have to weigh your cost and benefit tradeoffs. You might want to use more than one tool for a single prototype if you can see a way for multiple tools to work together and no single tool meets all your prototyping needs.

There are a number of other considerations to take into account when choosing your development tools, whether for design purposes or for final software development.

Familiarity.

Certainly familiarity counts for something—knowing a tool's capabilities and functionality can save you time and help you take advantage of it for your design.

Purpose.

Consider up front what you want to do with the prototype. Knowing your target audience and intended purpose can help clarify the tradeoffs among various tools.

Team size.

Consider also how many people on your development team will be working together on any particular prototype or software module. If more than one person is involved, choose tools that readily support integrating efforts from several sources.

Multiple application support.

Think about the need to support inter-application features. You might want to use the output from one tool as the input for another. If this will be important to you, choose tools accordingly.

Functionality support.

Consider the functionality you want to test. Software development tools have many features that can be isolated and evaluated in comparison, such as support for graphic capabilities, ability to interpret various user interactions, extendibility, and support for sound or video.

The criteria given here are simply a guideline for helping you evaluate your development tools. You might want to establish some standard evaluation criteria of your own, criteria that work consistently for the type of development you most often perform. You might consider establishing separate criteria for design/prototyping tools and for final software development tools.

If certain criteria are consistently important to you, you might want to jot down an informal evaluation list that you can reference at the start of each new project to help you quickly determine which tools might work the best for you. Additionally, you might want to keep a list of the advantages and disadvantages of particular tools as you use them, so that you can reference the list on later projects. In this case, you will probably want to categorize information so that you can evaluate similar characteristics of various tools. This will help later in comparisons.

The importance of selecting the right tools

Choosing the appropriate tools for development can significantly impact your design process. There are a number of advantages to taking the time at the beginning of your process to evaluate and select prototyping and design tools. Some of the reasons are that they:

Save development time and costs.

Using the right tools for development will surely save you time building your prototypes and your final software. There might be some initial investment costs to learning or acquiring new tools, but in the long run, the cost will be well worth it. Time and money spent up front will pay for themselves in the quality and success of your designs.

Prepare you for later work.

The process of using and evaluating various tools and techniques can be extremely productive for the project on which you are working and for later projects, as well. Even if you do not end up using each prototyping or development tool that you evaluate for your current project, by checking them out you learn something about them that can help you understand if they will be appropriate for a later design project. So do not feel that you are wasting time reviewing tools that you end up not using immediately—you are better prepared for future design.

Enable functionality in your prototype.

As you evaluate tools, you will explore the functions and features they offer. You might discover new ways of implementing them in your prototypes or the final software. Even more significantly, some features might help you to see your design in new ways, perhaps pointing out ways to enable or enhance your designs. They might even indicate features that you had previously thought were unavailable, or those that you did not realize could be used for the purposes of your designs. In using and evaluating various tools, you might get ideas for your designs that can help to make them better than you had originally thought possible.

Showcase the different purposes of different tools.

Reviewing and comparing different tools, particularly software development tools, will help you to evaluate which ones might be appropriate for certain designs and which for others. Different tools really do serve different purposes. You cannot assume that any tool will do for every prototype. Taking the time to look at more than one design tool will help you to know which tools make the most sense for you. At the same time, you might discover that you can combine available tools to build a prototype or system that is more robust than a single tool could provide. Only by looking at and thinking about different tools will you be able to determine the ones to use for your designs.

Support building better systems with better tools.

It really is true that your design will only be as good as the tools with which you design it. Clearly, sound design principles and strong creative ideas will also shape your design, but if you do not have the right tools with which to present your ideas, then your design process could be for naught. Even if you have excellent tools with which you are familiar, you might want to invest some time and energy in reviewing new tools, or talking with colleagues about the tools they use for various purposes. You might learn something about newly available tools, or how to use existing tools in new ways, which can help you in the future to develop excellent designs.

Steps for selecting the right tools

1. Identify what you want to do with the tools. Make a list of functions you want to support and any qualities you know you want in a tool.

2. Look at the tools with which you are already familiar. Decide if any of them are appropriate.

3. Research other tools available to you. Ask your colleagues, read current literature, and visit retail stores to see what tools you find. (You might want to conduct this research in your spare time, not necessarily only when you are in immediate need of prototyping and design tools.)

4. Establish some criteria for comparing the different tools. Build the same sample functional model using each of the tools.

5. Evaluate both the authoring capabilities (where you create your designs) and the runtime capabilities (where you play back or interact with your designs) of the tools.

6. Choose tools that run on an appropriate platform for the software being developed. It might be important that hardware support adequate prototyping tools.

7. Look for prototyping environments that support a range of development tools, such as graphics creation and manipulation tools.

8. Weigh the tradeoffs of system complexity with ease of use.

9. Check out the programming language that is supported. (Make sure that one is!) It should support basic constructs (variables, conditionals, and looping) and be extensible to link in other code modules. It is a benefit, of course, if the programmer is already familiarly with the language.

10. Determine which of the tools is most appropriate for your work. You might find that your familiar tools offer as much as the newly evaluated tools. If you believe your research has been thorough, then you might very well be best off with a familiar tool.

Hints/suggestions

- Select prototyping environments that support extension of existing prototypes and the integration of other system elements. Extension and integration can save you significant amounts of time.

- Look for alternate ways to make the most of tools with which you are familiar. Don't assume that you know everything there is to know about a tool. For example, consider how a tool that you've always used by yourself might contribute to the work of multiple designers. Also consider how using the tool differently might give you a different perspective on your prototype or final software. Even if you don't believe your current designs will ever change, chances are they will!

- Watch for useful tools. Look for relevant journal or newspaper reports and new software releases. Talk with your friends and colleagues about what they use for prototyping tools.

- When you have some available time, do some comparison studies of various tools you think you might want to learn more about. This information will be useful later and will save you from making the wrong tool decision.

Exercise task

Select appropriate tools for your software development project. Some of the things you should think about are:

- Do you know the platform you are developing for? What software tools are available for that platform?

- With which software development tools are you most familiar? How well-versed are you with these tools? How appropriate are they for your purposes?

- What do you intend to do with these tools? Are you testing parts of the design, or building an interactive prototype for use in user studies?

- Do you have specific end products or output in mind? Will you need to be able to accept certain input formats?

- Do you want to be able to reuse or extend your prototypes? This might be important to know when selecting tools.

Method 3: Using Software Prototyping Tools

Software construction toolsets that allow the programmer to quickly put together demonstrations of key concepts.

Software prototyping tools are on-line environments designed specifically to help you quickly create robust software. Different software prototyping environments provide different features. Some are intended for software engineering purposes—to help create, for instance, code that is as compact as possible, or targeted for a specific hardware platform. Others are specifically for developing a dynamic user interface.

For the purpose of user interface software design, you will certainly want to look for software prototyping tools that support a wide range of user inputs and interaction approaches. You need not, however, use only those that bill themselves as user interface design tools. A label can be deceptive; sometimes such tools offer little in the way of interactive support. And sometimes tools that are not labeled as user interface design tools offer a rich platform for interactive development. Use your own evaluation procedure to select software prototyping tools that are appropriate for your design needs (and see the previous section, Method 2: Selecting the Right Tools).

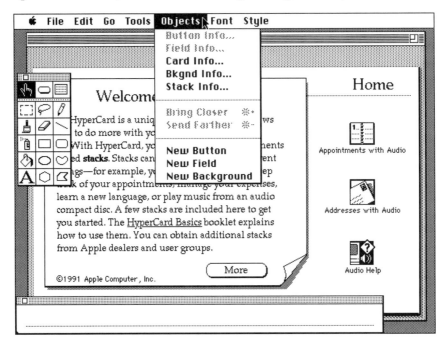

Figure 6.2 - HyperCard as a software prototyping tool.
Apple's HyperCard is a dynamic software prototyping environment which supports basic graphic design tools, easy definition
and editing of basic interactive elements such as buttons or text
fields, and an interactive message window for entering code
sequences. Code can also be included in the form of custom scripts
which can be associated with any interactive element. HyperCard
supports rapid prototyping of user interfaces which take advantage of simple Macintosh elements like clickable buttons, radio
buttons, check boxes, text regions, and sounds.

Creating software without writing code

Generally, software prototyping tools let you create software without having to write lengthy code to accomplish the task. The clear advantage is that you don't have to learn (or already know) a programming language to get your software to do the things you want it to do, as used to be the case if you wanted software to do anything! With the right tools you can, in most cases, quickly mock up your interactive designs. Many software prototyping environments do support programming language-type interfaces. Of those that do, many also allow you to achieve most of the same system functionality without having to write code at all. If you are a programmer, you will probably want to take advantage of an environment that allows you access to its features through a programmer's interface. However, if you are not an avid code writer, don't despair—you can accomplish a great deal without having to know a single programming command or structure.

Testing software designs

You can use software prototyping tools to test potentially complex system designs. You can get a feel for the complexity of the design, and even evaluate if the prototyping tool will also support your final software design.

Software prototyping tools offer an excellent platform for testing the complexity of your interactive designs. Once you take advantage of software prototyping tools to quickly put together an on-line version of your design, you can then show other design team members or potential users while it is still early in the development process. You can save days, weeks, or even months of time developing more complex software. Feedback you receive from other team members or potential users can help you to shape your design before you have invested significant time in the software itself.

Learning what works or doesn't work with your on-line designs as quickly as possible will not only save you time, it can help you to make decisions about how to present your software. You can use the feedback from user testing to decide how the software should really function; you won't have to deal with a programmer's lament that he or she has already spent so much time devoted to the way the system functions now.

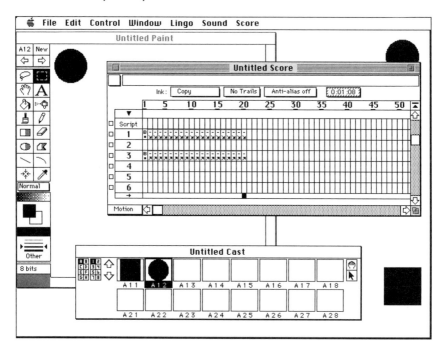

Figure 6.3 - Director as a software prototyping tool.
MacroMedia's Director is another multi-faceted software proto-typing environment with excellent graphic creation tools, support for custom scripting, and an animation-based interaction model complete with an organizational score and cast of characters. While Director does not directly support many of the interactive elements present on the Macintosh, its free-form structure supports whatever users attempt to create.

Integrating outside elements into your program

Another way that software prototyping tools are useful in the design process is that they often support the integration of elements of other prototypes or software. You might be able to import existing graphics from another software design, or use a scanner to bring hard-copy designs directly into your prototyping environment. Often sounds or videos created in other environments can be imported into software prototyping tools, as well. In this way, design work you did prior to your on-line activity can be transferred to your current design work. In some cases, you can even convert prototypes created in other design environments, and then import them into your current software prototyping tool. Or you can take advantage of components in previous designs, integrating them into your new design. Software prototyping tools are great construction kits for putting together a brand new design using elements from a variety of creative sources.

Timing of software prototyping

Take advantage of software prototyping tools as soon as you want to develop an on-line prototype. At the very least, you should, at that point, evaluate if software prototyping tools can work for you. You might want to consider this early in the design phase, after you have designed off-line system maps or flipbooks, for example. That way you can more thoroughly check out the look and feel of your system on-line than is possible with the paper prototypes. You might want to wait to introduce software prototyping tools until some of your early on-line explorations are done, or wait until you have drafted system requirements or begun to piece together your various graphic, sound, and video data.

There is no harm in starting on-line prototyping early and bringing in the pieces as they are available. You can also continue to use software prototyping tools during your final software development, even if you do not plan to develop your final software in the prototyping environment. As your system or application progresses, use software prototyping tools to support small studies or experiments, particularly those that would otherwise require long amounts of time in your target software development process. Whenever you are still testing the appropriateness of the design itself, software prototyping tools are excellent ways to save time and still build designs that can provide you with significant feedback.

The importance of using software prototyping tools

As noted previously, there are a number of excellent reasons to take advantage of software prototyping tools. In summary, software prototyping tools are important because with them you can:

Demonstrate the system's capabilities as early as possible.

Particularly when you can find software prototyping tools that allow you to quickly mockup your interactive elements, you can demonstrate functionality of your user interface software on-line long before you might otherwise be able to using more conventional software development processes. You can therefore present what appears to be a working version of your software to potential users or any other audience whose feedback might be critical in influencing the direction of your system.

Test components of the system.

While there might be times when you choose one for other reasons, the most consistent advantage of a software prototyping tool is that it supports rapid prototyping; you can quickly put together the various components of your system. The prototyping tool will also offer organization and presentation benefits. However, the main advantage over a conventional programming language should be the speed with which you can put together system components.

Keep in mind that you make a tradeoff when you choose to use a prototyping tool: you are more confined by the tool model than you might be when using an open-ended programming language for development.

Integrate graphical components.

Software prototyping tools can be excellent platforms for quickly and dynamically integrating the visual elements of your design. Many software prototyping environments offer a range of graphical tools with which you can enhance or combine your screen visuals. Typical programming languages alone do not support such functionality. Having graphical editing tools directly in the software prototyping environment can prove useful as your designs develop, even if you do not think that the designs are important at the start of the process. If you find it necessary to alter your graphical elements, having visual editing tools available for easy access within your software prototyping environment can simplify your development and save you time.

Obtain consensus from others.

Because you will be able to use software prototyping tools to quickly put together parts of your design, you can show these design elements to others early in the development process. This will enable you to achieve consensus from appropriate parties, such as potential users or your management. Using software prototyping tools to put together something you can discuss together can be critically helpful to the design process.

Steps for using software prototyping tools

1. Gain a basic understanding of how to use the prototyping tool: work through tutorials, read introductory manuals, and play with any available examples.

2. Check out the programming language or extensions that are supported. Even if you don't know whether you will use the language, a basic understanding of what it does will help you

to know when you might want to use it and whether it is appropriate.

3.   Look at a range of designs that have been built using this tool. They will help you to understand the kinds of work this tool is capable of. You might be so lucky as to have such samples immediately available to you through colleagues or other sources; if not, you might want to invest some time researching. Sometimes you can contact the tool developer for a list of works created with the tool that you might evaluate.

4.   Before you build your "real" prototype, build small sample programs (such as a calculator) to test the tool. Using software prototyping tools for early on-line explorations can serve two purposes: it teaches you about the tool itself, and it lets you explore preliminary concepts for your software.

5.   Organize your prototype before you simply dive in and build it. Often prototyping tools have metaphors for interaction. Thinking about how your prototype can take advantage of this model, or how it will have to get around it, will help you with your overall design.

6.   As you build your prototype, take advantage of any development or debugging features the tool has to offer.

Hints/suggestions

•   Understand the features and limitations of the tools you use. You might want to focus on one aspect of your design because your prototyping tool can best support its functionality. Likewise, you might need to minimize another function if you cannot easily implement it in your tool's environment.

•   Be creative with your prototyping tools. Learn how to take advantage of the features offered, or coerce them into behaving in alternative ways. Talk with colleagues about the tricks they use to get the tools to respond in needed ways.

- Learn to combine different prototyping tools to meet your needs. Macintosh prototyping tools such as HyperCard and MacroMind's Director will allow you to launch other applications, or to import other file formats for use within applications developed in their environments.

- Remember that you are building prototypes and not full working systems. Every feature need not work for you to get your point across. When your prototyping tool does not support necessary implementation capabilities, use creative alternatives. These might include "hard-wired" segments that simply animate a planned interactive segment, or might even be still graphic frames that can serve as a background while you describe an intended feature.

Exercise task

Design and build at least one on-line prototype using software prototyping tools. You will probably want to take advantage of your evaluation from the exercise in the previous section, Method 2: Selecting the Right Tools, to identify which tools to use. These should be some of your considerations:

- Which tool is most appropriate for your prototype? Will a single tool meet your needs, or might you need to combine more than one tool?

- Do you know enough about the tool's features to build your prototype? You might want to explore new features with which you were previously unfamiliar.

- Can you use elements from other designs that were created with this software prototyping tool? What about elements from other pieces of software? Reuse whenever you can.

- Can you build small sections of the prototype that can later be linked together? There is usually no need to develop prototypes in any particular order.

- What kinds of place holders can you use to keep from having to address particular details at inopportune times?

   Do you have access to all hardware and software functionality you need from this prototyping tool? If not, you might need to design creative alternatives.

   If there is more than one way to implement something with this tool, do you know which makes better sense for your design?

Software Prototypes in User Studies

The previous sections in this chapter discuss the importance and use of software prototypes in user studies in a general way, looking at the overall advantages of all kinds of prototypes, not simply on-line ones. The rest of this chapter specifically discusses software prototypes and user studies: why to use them, the possible implications of using software prototypes in user studies, and hints for designing and building prototypes that are to be used in user studies.

Value of software prototypes in user studies

Since you are ultimately developing software, using software prototypes for your user studies can be especially valuable. While off-line prototypes will help you to get at initial design questions and are extremely useful in their own right, on-line prototypes can help you obtain more design-specific feedback from your study participants and potential users.

In almost all cases, your users will respond more naturally to software prototypes than to off-line prototypes. Users provide feedback that is more appropriate for your design when they are testing software prototypes that represent the target system as closely as possible As you move your designs on-line, you will address, either by choice or necessity, the details of your software prototype that will be the same for your final software. Issues that were fuzzy or misunderstood in earlier off-line studies will no longer be questionable. Users will see graphics of comparable size and resolution to the final images; they will hear sound and observe video that are unavailable in off-line prototypes; image color and quality will no longer be in question. Clearly, these are details with which you did not want to concern yourself in earlier off-line designs, but as your design progresses, feedback on these issues becomes critical to the success of your software.

Conducting user studies with software prototypes can also help support conditions that are truer to the actual system you are building, particularly when the software prototypes run on the target platform. Issues such as response times can be more accurately tested with potential users, both in terms of whether speeds are adequate and whether feedback given to the user is appropriate. Likewise, if your software prototype supports interaction with the same input devices that will be used in your final software, you can gain valuable feedback on whether the devices are appropriate and if users can adequately manipulate them. These platform-based concerns can make or break your final software, as well.

Implications of building prototypes for user studies

There are, of course, a number of implications for your designs when you intend to use software prototypes in user studies. Users cannot be expected to know the delicate condition of your prototypes. In many cases, you don't want to let them know that your prototypes are not real working software! Prototypes used for user studies or testing purposes need to be more robust than those built for design or demonstration purposes.

Your study participants, like it or not, will be hard on your prototypes. They will not necessarily know how to interact with them, and might not identify interaction methods or feedback mechanisms that you thought completely clear in your design process. More importantly, they will try to interact with your system in ways that you did not anticipate. While you cannot expect to be prepared for every single action a user might take, you should attempt to make your system as flexible as possible. Anticipate that the user might select the "wrong" button, or try to slide a control bar in an unintended way.

Include feedback for inappropriate activity in your prototype design. This doesn't mean that during the study you should be prepared to point out immediately the intended interaction. On the contrary, you should sit back and watch for what the user thinks is the intended interaction. Designing your system to anticipate as many misunderstandings as possible will actually help you to conduct studies that give you the most valuable feedback on the success of your user interface.

One way to prepare for such user misunderstandings is to analyze your software prototype with the user in mind. If you will be using your prototype for user studies or testing, identify what you believe are the most important functionalities. Think about how the user might see your software for these specific functions. Come up with at least one alternative for carrying out each important feature, no matter how bizarre it might seem to you or how sure you are that users will know what to do. Remember that you know much more about this software than the typical user, and someone without your knowledge could easily make the mistake that you think is wildly unlikely.

If the user does make an unexpected move, your software should provide appropriate feedback. Better than simply pointing out that the action was invalid, provide instruction for the expected interaction. Offering a system beep at a "wrong" response is useful, since it indicates to the user that the input was received but could not be interpreted. A dialog box explaining what the system thought the user was trying to do is more useful. You do not, of course, want to bombard your user with dialog boxes for every action. You will have to use your best judgment in anticipating the appropriate feedback, and then be prepared to change your approach based on the feedback you actually receive during your studies.

Another way to think about your design is to plan ahead for any feature that appears to be provided by your prototype but that you know is not going to be active for a particular study. Put handles in your prototype that catch a user's interactions with the inactive feature, then inform the user that the feature is not yet implemented. This feedback might be as direct as a dialog box message that says, "Sorry, this feature is not yet available." Depending on the nature of your design, you might want to communicate this message in some other way. The important aspect is that you give users the feedback necessary to know what is going on, to discover how to interact with your prototype, and to avoid feeling confused so that they will want to continue.

Hints for prototypes in user studies

Tell users about limitations in the software only when necessary. It will throw off the accuracy of your findings if you tell the user everything you expect to happen before it actually does. Start by letting the user think that more of the system works than actually does. As specific problems arise, you can point out that something is not yet active. If you tell users too much at the beginning, you might discourage them from trying all the feature that are active.

Test and evaluate only those concepts that will truly be transferred to the final system. Often users will start down the wrong path of giving you feedback, thinking you are interested in a particular aspect of the software that is there only as a place holder. Don't be afraid to put the user on the right path, before you've spent significant time listening to input that cannot help you. Try to ignore irrelevant feedback.

Consider that there could be a need to reset or restart initial conditions of your software prototype from study to study. Your prototype does not have to be perfect, and there is nothing wrong with planning to reset these conditions at the end of each user session. (However, don't do so in front of users and give the impression that the software is not "real" or working.)

When you aren't sure which features might be interpreted in certain ways but you won't have time to run many versions of user studies, you might want to use "dry runs" to get the big bugs out early. In these cases, bring in colleagues or friends (who aren't involved in the design itself but might not be appropriate study subjects otherwise) and let them play with your software for a bit. These people can help you to identify significant problems that weren't apparent to you because you know too much about the design. You can then revise your software before user studies begin. Be sure to interpret carefully the input from these dry runs. You don't want to make a change that isn't truly merited before you've had adequate feedback from a balance of users—which is precisely why you are to conduct the study in the first place.

Preparing for the Actual Software

At some point you will move from prototyping to building your final software. While this book does not talk specifically about software development, the following guidelines can help you prepare for the switch to building your actual software.

1. Understand the differences in the actual system and the prototypes. Review both hardware and software requirements and re-examine your priorities. Often elements that were important to building and testing prototypes might not be critical in the final system. Also, factors such as cost and speed might have been ignored in the prototyping phases.

2. Understand how any differences in the system will affect the user interface design. Hardware differences might mean alternate input or output devices are necessary. Software differences can affect system speed or integration.

3. Reuse anything and everything you can! Graphics, code, and even algorithms all are candidates for reuse. Leverage mate-

rials from early on-line prototypes or studies. Plan to do so as early as possible in the process.

4. Explore translation alternatives. Look at tool environments on all target platforms. Talk with others who might have some experience. When you are writing code segments, isolate machine dependencies (bitmaps, environment variables, and so forth) to ease portability concerns later.

5. Plan to iterate. Schedule generous time for user testing and redesign. Assume the worst; it can only get better!

Chapter 7

Usability Testing

What Is Usability Testing?

Usability testing, also called user testing, is the process of evaluating software by having targeted users actually work with it (or a subset of it) in a test situation. It is the most widely practiced user-centered design technique. User testing can help you see where your software works as expected and where there are significant problems. Some problems will be obvious, as when many users have trouble with the same parts of the user interface. While it will not always be possible to pinpoint all problems, user testing will at least indicate inconsistencies in your design, or help you better understand the expectations of your users. User testing is valuable because it guides you to significant improvements in your software.

Usability testing can be formally or informally conducted. Formal ways, which use rigid testing structures, are oriented toward gathering statistics that can be analyzed to show behavior patterns or significant results. Many papers and texts present methods for conducting this formal type of usability testing. The techniques for user testing presented in the following sec-

tions, however, are a group of informal methodologies. While they don't necessarily lead to statistically formal findings, they can still provide valuable
information about the functionality and features of your software system.

Formal versus Informal Testing

It is important in all usability testing to get feedback from target users in as
"real" an environment as possible. Formal methods are not needed to obtain
valuable feedback as long as you follow this basic approach. You do not need
to set up regulated, controlled environments with large numbers of test subjects to generate useful findings. Of course, there might be times when you
do want to conduct the more formal types of tests; by no means do I want to
discourage you from doing so.

Much of the time, however, you will conduct tests in less than ideal circumstances. I refer to this kind of testing as informal because you are, to varying
degrees, "making do" when the perfect testing situation doesn't exist. Imper-
fect situations might be a result of an incomplete system, or no access to a
realistic setting, or an inability to recruit test participants who are similar to
target users. Still, knowing the drawbacks of your particular testing situation
can help you tailor the test accordingly and achieve extremely useful results.

Establishing Test Goals and a Plan

In planning and conducting your user tests, it is important to understand
what you are trying to learn about the system, not simply to present it to
your users. It isn't enough to place people in front of your system and say,
"Use it." Or to ask, "What do you think?" This approach will not yield as
much information about your system as will guiding test participants to really
use the system.

You should prepare for a usability test by establishing goals, and then generating a plan based on those goals. Give the users tasks to perform that will
direct them through the system, and that will motivate them to use the sys-

tem in a real-world way. This will give you the information you need about the problems and successes of your system.

Have each participant complete the same tasks to give you a basis for comparison among users. Examine different users' approaches to the same tasks to look for problems as well as see where things seem to work. You can refer to the results of the user tests to identify problems and make recommendations for how to solve them.

The Timing of Usability Testing

Even though usability testing is the most widely practiced form of user-centered design, it is still not practiced as often as it could be. User testing can happen at any time—it need not wait until a software product is ready to ship. You can apply user testing methods during early phases of development as extended user studies. You can combine some of the early user study methods presented in Chapter 3 with the usability testing techniques here to devise your own user-based approaches to design and evaluation.

Usability testing should not happen only toward the end of the development process or wait until a completely working prototype exists. It is valuable throughout the design process. The purpose of user testing is to obtain feedback to make the software better; your testing will be for naught if you wait until the end of the process when you no longer have the time or system flexibility to adequately incorporate what you learn. Another kind of testing, quality control testing, can (and should) happen toward the end of the development cycle so you can evaluate how successful the software is for potential users.

Determining the Number of Tests to Run

The usability testing procedures described in the following sections do not provide a formula for determining how many users must be tested before significant results can be realized. In informal usability testing, there is no science to determining how many users to test. There is a rule of thumb, however: test enough subjects to gather useful information. This does not necessarily mean hundreds or even tens of users; it can be as few as five or six, depending on the nature of the software or problem you are testing.

Critical problems typically become evident after test sessions with just a couple of users. Less obvious problems, or issues that might be problematic to some users and not to others, will take more participant sessions to become evident. With time and experience you will get a feel for how many users to test. In any case, I am not arguing for always testing few users. You have to be sure that you test enough users so that the results:

- Include significant information.

- Eliminate the possibility of chance results.

- Eliminate any biases among the users.

Usability Testing—Part of User-Oriented Design

Usability testing is an integral part of user-oriented design. However, it alone does not constitute true user-oriented software design. User-oriented design involves target users throughout the design and development process. Usability testing toward the end of the design process is, of course, better than no user involvement at all. But don't call yourself a user-oriented software designer because you happen to show your software to a few potential users before you ship it out. This chapter presents critical methodologies for usability testing. These techniques are most effective when combined with the design approaches presented in other chapters, and can be adapted to meet your personal needs as long as you keep the basic principles in mind.

The Advantages of Usability Testing

The various techniques of usability testing are critical to the overall design process because they:

Indicate potential users' reactions to the system.

The most important aspect of usability tests is that they give you an opportunity to see and interpret potential users' reactions to your system or application. Bringing in objective users to use your design can be an irreplaceable way to stage a reality check. Even if you have used other user-oriented techniques in the development of your software, usability testing can expose a variety of ways to improve your system because target users will always have something to say about your design.

Show you system problems or flaws.

The type of usability testing techniques explained here are probably best suited to highlight problems in your current design. Identifying these problems is the reason you conduct usability tests—when you identify the ways people have problems using your product, you can refine your design and make it better. These changes serve as the bridge for the next iteration of your prototype design.

Show you where the system works well.

Usability testing also supports the successful aspects of your system. When you find that test participants are able to complete various tasks successfully and use system features without problems, then you have validation of the usability of those aspects of your system.

Help you evaluate design issues and conflicts.

Usability testing can be particularly helpful in lending support to design decisions, especially those that might have been somewhat questionable or controversial among team members. Seeing objective, unbiased users support one design idea over another can be an extremely convincing argument for following that approach. The approach to take might become evident through an overwhelmingly positive attitude toward a system feature or element, or in repetitive user problems with a specific feature or element. In either case, seeing one user after another have the same reaction is persuasive (and can be presented to the "non-believers" through back-to-back video clips).

Provide design ideas through user suggestions.

Participants in usability tests will typically not only tell you what you want to learn about the existing system, but they can be an excellent source for design ideas, as well. In the course of trying to complete the tasks of a usability test, users will often point out how they would prefer to see a feature or element. If users do not offer their suggestions unprompted, be sure to ask them what they are thinking about during tests, and at the end of the test ask them what they expected or preferred. Don't pass up an opportunity for first-hand design ideas!

Give you a means of comparing multiple users.

Usability testing allows you to compare the interactions of users. This comparison can be critical in understanding the relative importance of a test participant's feedback. While having just one participant come in and use your software can reveal interesting results, this would yield the opinions of only a single person. It is important to solicit responses from enough participants so that you can complete this comparison and be sure your findings are truly reflective of your system.

Give you support for further design work.

Users' reactions to your software can provide the information necessary to indicate that your design is not only usable, but needed and wanted. This can be the impetus necessary to decide to go further with the software (or it can be a clear indication that the current approach will not work and an overhaul in the design is needed).

Encourage user support.

One of the best side effects of usability testing is that you establish a rapport with potential users of your system. Participants in your usability tests can become strong supporters of your software. Sometimes this is so because they are simply happy to have been asked for their opinions; other times it is because they see that you are building a product they really need. In any case, having advocates of your product from your potential user population is an added benefit of usability testing.

How to Design and Perform Usability Tests

There are a number of factors to consider when organizing your usability tests. They can differ significantly from one another—they are not as simple as sitting users down in front of the system and asking them directly to tell you how you should change it to make it better. There are some considerations you can make that will help guide you in determining the tasks for the test, the qualifications for your participants, the length of time for each testing session, and other related factors. These issues are presented in the following sections.

Examine the goals of your system

The best way to understand how to structure and run your usability tests is to know ahead of time what you are trying to get out of them. You can do this by thinking about the goals of your system. Ask yourself what the main purpose is of this system, and what the basic tasks are that you want users to be able to accomplish.

Your goals might be quite general, especially if you are conducting tests early in the design process and you are exploring basic navigation or layout of the software. On the other hand, if you are trying to understand detailed information, such as if users perceive the subtle messages in your iconography, you might have very specific goals. Goals will differ from one testing situation to the next, so it is important that you think about goals for each version of the software you want to test.

Evaluate the state of your system

Another factor that might influence what you are able to include in your test is the actual condition of your software. Particularly if you are testing a prototype, parts of the system might not be functional. It's okay to conduct a usability test on a partial system. You will, of course, want to be careful to plan the test so that you steer users away from the portions of your system that are not active. If need be, you can tell them that this is only a prototype and they should ignore certain missing functionality. However, depending on the users and the software, telling them this might negatively influence their interaction, so tell them only if you absolutely must. Instead, try structuring your tasks to focus on the features that are available that you do want to test to obtain the most valuable feedback.

Assess the capabilities and availability of your testers

Knowing what you can realistically accomplish during your usability tests will help you to understand what you can expect to learn from them and how to structure them. Look at what resources are available to you for conducting the test. How many people will be able to participate in the tests? Who will those people be? How much time do they have available? What are their skills and experience? All of these factors can come into play when you are planning your testing sessions.

While the ideal situation is to be able to select testers who meet your exact testing criteria, in the real world it is unlikely that you will be able to fit your ideal. You can still make the most of the testing sessions if you critically assess the abilities of your testers and structure the tests to take advantage of those abilities.

Consider which and how many users to include

Your test participants can also be critical in helping you determine how much you will be able to accomplish during your testing. Think about how you will recruit test participants and how you will compensate them. In some situations, finding representative users is not an easy task. Product confidentiality, limited funds, and not really knowing who your users will be are issues that might make it difficult to find an adequate number of test participants. If you cannot find truly representative users, you have a choice:

- You can find a sampling of other participants from whom you can still learn valuable information. For instance, you could change the nature of the test tasks and then hypothesize about how your findings might relate to the actual system and target users.

- Or you can use the few representative users available to you, but risk not obtaining enough feedback to get sound, unbiased results.

Understanding what you will be able to expect from your test participants can help you better understand and structure your usability tests.

Determine the setting for your tests

Consider where you will hold your usability tests and under what conditions. The availability of any equipment necessary to support the test, an appropriate room for testing (quiet, with adequate space, light, and privacy), video or other recording equipment, and accessibility for your participants all might come into play when planning your testing sessions. Understanding the criteria that the environment for your tests must meet and finding a setting to meet these criteria are important considerations in planning and conducting your user tests.

Spend enough time and include enough users

As with early user studies, make your testing sessions worthwhile by being sure to include enough users with whom you spend adequate time (see Chapter 3 for more complete details). While there is no exact formula for knowing how much time to spend or how many users are enough, there are some rules of thumb to follow.

- A testing session should be at least 45 minutes; any less doesn't really give participants enough time to formulate opinions about your software or its features.

- A testing session should not be longer than 1-1/2 to 2 hours; beyond that, participants are too bored or tired to contribute useful information.

- Fewer than five users probably does not comprise enough of a sample to really get useful results.

- Time spent testing any more than 20 participants probably will not shed significantly new information and will therefore not be worth your time.

With experience you will get a feel for how long to allocate for various tasks or how many users to include. Project constraints might also limit the total time you can spend or the number of participants you can include. Being aware of your constraints and expectations can help you make the most of your testing sessions.

Document the testing sessions

Record what goes on during the testing sessions. Use written notes, audio or videotape recordings, or a buddy system where others can observe or record findings to adequately document user responses and feedback. These records will help you later to better understand what went on during the tests. They also might provide content for reports or presentations based on your findings.

Understand what usability testing can do for you

While usability testing is a valuable way to obtain feedback from target users of your software, it will not solve all your design problems or necessarily provide answers to all your questions. Knowing what you expect to learn from your usability tests ahead of time can help you make the most of the time you spend with your testers.

Participants can point out what is incomprehensible about your system, or if they don't like the available functions. They cannot, however, always tell you what they do want or what would work better. Sometimes you will receive as many different suggestions for alternatives as you have participants. You will have to make sense of users' responses and determine the best way to resolve any problems.

Listening to your users is important, but you still have to apply design and problem-solving skills and come up with alternative solutions yourself. You might even have to start again from scratch depending on participants' reactions. Don't assume that holding usability tests is enough and that you will be done with the project as soon as the testing is complete!

Know when to test

Usability testing can be extremely helpful in addressing the issues presented previously in the Advantages of Usability Testing section. Recognizing the value of user testing and when it is appropriate to conduct user tests in your design process can help you make the most of testing and lend the most support to your design effort. Still, usability testing is not the solution to all your design problems, and simply conducting a usability test will not necessarily produce helpful results. Knowing when usability testing can be helpful and when it is simply adding time to your design process can aid you not just in carrying out your usability tests, but in completing your design.

Method 1: Designing a User Test

Understanding how the user interface you are developing can be evaluated, and making a plan to adequately conduct that evaluation.

Before you can put your users in front of your software to obtain the valuable information that they will impart, spend some significant effort planning for and designing your usability testing sessions. While it might seem that the most important parts of usability testing—and possibly the entire user-centered design process—are the usability tests themselves, the usability tests are only as good as they are designed. In designing the tests, you will set the stage for the type of information that you will gather, and the influence it will have on your ensuing designs.

Establish goals for the test

The first things to consider are the purpose of your software and the goals of the test. Think about what you want your users to accomplish with your software. The goals set the foundation for what you will ask users to accomplish during the testing session and help you configure the test to focus their responses.

Your goals might be general in nature: to determine whether users are able to understand the basic functionality of the system, or whether they can grasp the general navigation approach. General goals are typical of usability tests conducted early in the design process.

If user testing comes later in the design process, you might have more detailed goals, such as: to determine whether users know to use the menus to find a certain feature, or whether they are able to adequately express themselves in a system that solicits user input. The goals you have for your software largely determine your goals for usability testing. This is why it is so important to understand the specific goals for your current design when you begin the user testing process.

One way to help determine your testing goals is to evaluate the system your-self. Evaluate the system from the point of view of your target users—not necessarily the structure or design of your system (although if the structure is something you want users to be able to understand, this might come into play in your evaluation). Use the software, or intermediate design, if that's what you are testing, as you expect that your users will. Follow the steps in the order that you think others will. You will begin to see what kinds of expectations you have for the software and your users.

Keep in mind that you know much more about this design than your users will; while you know which step to take next, your users might not. As part of this evaluation process, think about what types of things might confuse your users, and what they might do instead of the "correct" choice. Think-ing about potential unexpected responses, as well as thinking about what you want users to do, will help you set your goals for the test.

Devise tasks for the test

Once your goals are well understood, the next step is to come up with tasks that you will ask participants to accomplish that you hope will contribute information toward your test goals. You will most likely not want to come right out and ask users what they think of a certain feature or screen element, since this might cause them to think about this feature or element in an unnatural way. Instead, provide them with a real-world task that will intro-duce them to the feature or element.

The purpose of the task is to get your participants to act as they would if they were trying to use the system to accomplish the actual task on the actual system. Although usability tests are a somewhat staged production, make the test as much as possible like the situations in which you expect people will use your system. By doing this, you will learn the most useful informa-tion about your software, information that can help you shape a truly usable and successful product.

Determine the environment for the test

In order for the user tests to be of maximum effectiveness, the sessions should parallel as closely as possible the environment and setting in which the target software will be used. Whenever feasible, plan to conduct the tests in the same environment in which you think the final system will be used.

For example, if you are developing software for a desktop platform in an office environment, conduct tests in a similar office environment. If you cannot reproduce the environment exactly, try to come as close as possible. If you are designing software for public information kiosks to be placed at strategic locations around a shopping mall, strongly consider holding your tests in the mall itself. If that is not possible, try to simulate the noisy, distracting environment. Creating a setting as similar as possible to that of your intended environment can help you uncover information critical to the working of your software or your user's thought process that would be lost in another testing environment.

Decide how to record the test

Consider how you will record each session. Will you be able to use audio or videotape? Will you have a second observer present who will be able to concentrate on recording the session while you run it? Even if you are able to use some sort of recording medium or another person is available, it is probably a good idea to take some form of written notes yourself.

Don't let your note taking distract from your ability to conduct the tests; think carefully about how you will record what goes on. Still, while note taking can be distracting, it is often the most effective way to mark the events of the test session. When you are in the process of conducting the test, you will have critical thoughts that you will want to capture for fear of forgetting them later.

One approach that can help you take notes is to prepare a worksheet ahead of time and have a copy of the worksheet available for each test session. Structure the worksheet around the key goals of the test or the tasks themselves. Then, when you are taking notes, you will only have to jot down the results in the designated areas, not write an explanation of the entire situation. You will need room on the worksheet for unanticipated findings, as well, but at least most of your note taking will be recorded within your planned organization.

Establish the need for post-test interviews or questionnaires

Think about whether you will follow each test with an interview, or have participants fill out a prepared questionnaire. Remember to conduct the test sessions themselves without intervening too much. During the test don't ask the user for long explanations, and don't discuss topics that you think are important in determining a better approach to your design. However, once all the tasks are completed, take advantage of the opportunity to understand the participant's thoughts and reactions by asking questions. A post-test interview is an excellent way to find out what the participants were thinking or to test new ideas.

When you are planning your test, determine if you will "debrief" users after each test session. Consider whether a verbal interview is appropriate, or whether you will have the participant fill out a written questionnaire.

- Verbal interviews provide an opportunity to clarify a response or probe further on an interesting issue. However, some people might not respond as openly in a discussion format.

- Questionnaires allow users to express themselves without fear of being judged. However, they limit you to the predetermined topics. Questionnaires are also beneficial when you want to ask participants to rate responses. For example, you might include a scale of 1-to-10, where 1 means "Strongly Agree" and 10 means "Strongly Disagree." Scaled responses lend themselves well to more statistical analysis of your results.

In any case, it will help you to think about either a verbal interview or a questionnaire ahead of time and to outline the topics for discussion or create the questionnaire form along with your tasks for the test.

Establish the timing of the test

You do not have to wait until you have working software to conduct a usability test. Usability testing is appropriate early on in the design process, when you have developed a storyboard, flipbook, or other prototype for which you would like user feedback on your design. You can also be planning for your usability tests throughout your design process. Even if you are not able to test as often as you might like, make note of any important issues that come up that you will want to be sure to address later, when you do have an opportunity to test.

Usability testing can be an excellent way to resolve design problems, particularly among design team members who have opposing viewpoints. Gauging users reactions to alternative approaches might help you decide which is the more appropriate design to follow. And, of course, be sure to conduct usability tests when you do have a working version of your software, before you consider it a final product. A design that you think is flawless may appear different to the eyes of your users. Your usability tests will introduce you to issues that you didn't even know existed; but once acknowledged and resolved, those issues will improve your product immensely.

```
                      AMEX Project
                 Usability Testing Plan

General Goal: People with access to a Macintosh will
be able to fill out the form on their desktops and
send it from there to Am Ex

Goals:
  • See that people can generally navigate through
    the system.  See if we need to have a startup or
    central organization screen.

  • Check all necessary information before an order
    is submitted.

  • Iconography representative of functionality.

  • Clear wording of prompts and commands.

  • Adequate response time and feedback.

  • Obvious separation of inquiry v. reservation.

  • Clear definition and role of the AmEx profile.

Check the following specific features:
      On the "schedule" screen, current
        departure/arrival layout
      The "flexible" option
      Primary traveler v. companion(s)
      More than one destination, hotels and cars
      International travel
      Rental car or other transportation info
      Typing in information v. choose from a list
      Help system
```

Figure 7.1 Test goals and subsequent tasks. This document, on the next three pages, presents preliminary usability testing goals and the tasks generated from these goals for an on-line travel request system designed by the Stanford University Data Center.

Any features missing which people would like.

Find out if the on-line system is better than the current process.

Tasks:

1. You will be attending a seminar in Seattle from April 20 - 24. You would like to make airline reservations and get some information about hotels and rental cars. Use this on-line system to do this.

2. In June, you will be traveling to Toronto to give a talk at a conference. You would like to arrange the trip, and see how much it would cost to bring your spouse and 2 kids along with you. Your conference is June 10 - 13, and you would like to stay on in Toronto until June 16 to enjoy a vacation with them. You will need a hotel room that will sleep all of you, as well as a large enough rental car. Use the system to plan your trip.

3. In May you will be making an "east coast tour". On May 5 you are scheduled to talk in Boston early in the morning. On May 7 you have a talk in Philadelphia, and on May 8 and 9 you must be in New York. You want to fly from San Francisco, but return to San Jose on May 10. You will need a hotel and rental car in every city. Use the system to make the arrangements.

```
4. You are planning a business trip to Santa Fe, New
Mexico some time this summer, probably in July, but
you are flexible if it affects the cost of the trip.
You have never been to Santa Fe, but have heard a
few things about it that affect your needs for this
trip.  Firstly, friends have told you that it is
difficult to fly there from the Bay Area (you may
have to switch planes or fly out of Oakland or San
Jose rather than SFO, and you probably will fly into
Albequerque rather than Santa Fe directly).
Secondly, there is a wonderful hotel in the main
square where you would like to stay, but you have
forgotten the name of the hotel and you do not know
how expensive it is.  Finally, you hear it is not
the kind of place you want a rental car, and would
like to know what other transportation options are
available to you, both from the airport to your
hotel and then within the city of Santa Fe.  Use the
system to plan your trip.
```

The importance of designing a user test

Taking adequate time and energy to design your user tests is well worth the effort you will expend. A well-designed user test can help you to:

Set up conditions that will identify problems with the functions or operations of the system.

Planning the appropriate tasks for your usability testing sessions can be critical in achieving results that truly help you evolve your design. Understand the conditions in both the test content and test environment that will most likely lead you to useful findings. Well-designed tests can help you find problems that will lead to critical changes in your design. Less well-designed tests might simply take your time and provide only marginally important results.

Provide objective feedback for the design team.
In the process of designing your user tests, you will evaluate your design and assess the goals of your system. This process allows you to provide objective feedback to your design team, both in the course of planning the test and then in gathering the subject information. Remember that everyone's goal is to build a better product, so being as objective as possible is the best thing for everyone.

Consider direction for further development.
Designing usability tests can help you understand the strengths and weaknesses of your system. This process can provide the basis for any further development on your design, both in the results yielded from the testing sessions and the structure of your test plan. When questionable areas arise, make note of them. Do the same for elements that receive positive attention. Using the test-planning stage as a foundation for further design makes it doubly valuable to the development process.

Make the most of your time with potential users.
Taking time to plan your user tests might seem like an unnecessary drain on your resources, but the little time you spend up front organizing your test sessions will pay off many times over. We often get little time with our potential users, because of restricted schedules or participant availability. Take advantage of the time you do have with these users; you cannot expect to invite them back repeatedly as you change the direction of your desired feedback. Planning the user tests will enable you to truly make the most of the limited time you have with your users.

Steps for designing a user test

1. Evaluate the prototype you will be testing. Use the prototype yourself or have someone else demonstrate the system. What are the tasks the user must accomplish? Where are the potential problem areas?

2. Make a list of the general test areas and related goals for the test.

3. Think of a task that the user can accomplish that will objectively evaluate each item in your list. Make the tasks as "real" as possible.

4. Order the tasks logically, according the way the user might be most likely to conduct these tasks when really using the system.

5. Consider using post-test interviews or questionnaires to evaluate results.

6. Determine the length of each session and how you will record results.

7. Schedule the test and recruit subjects.

Hints/suggestions

- Leave plenty of time between tests, usually at least half an hour. This will give you time to complete your documentation of the test, reset any system conditions, prepare for the next user, and just take a break. Usability testing can be extremely tiring, and short breaks between tests will help.

- Do not plan too many tests in one day. Even with breaks between tests, you probably will not want to spend an entire day testing. Four-to-six tests in a single day is probably all you should aim for to keep from losing interest or energy in conducting tests. Spread out testing sessions over a period of days.

- If necessary, run short sample tests to understand what you can hope to learn from your tests. These "tests of the tests" might help you design your tasks for the actual tests.

- Plan to let users struggle for a little bit—you will learn from their troubles.

In designing the tasks you will present to users, tell them only as much as they need to know to complete each task. Usually, you will provide more motivational information on what they should hope to accomplish rather than an explanation of system functionality.

```
                          AMEX Project
                  Post-Test Interview Questions

     1. Did you like having an on-line system for making
        travel arrangements?

     2. In general, did you find you could navigate
        through this system successfully?  If so, what
        made it this way?  If not, what might have
        helped?

     3. Was the information grouped in logical ways?

     4. Did you think there was any difference between
        requesting information and actually reserving
        a trip?

     5. Did you know that there were required information
        to be included before a request could be
        successfully submitted?

     6. Did you know what an American Express profile
        was?  Did you imagine you'd have one?  Did you
        want to complete one?

     Ask about:
             • iconography
             • wording
             • response time/feedback
             • typing in information
             • "flexible" scheduling
             • international travel
             • additional travelers
             • missing features?
             • help
```

Figure 7.2 A debriefing questionnaire. These questions were designed for interviewing users after the Stanford travel request system usability tests. (see Figure 7.1)

Exercise task

Design a usability test for your system in its current state. The more you focus on designing a realistic usability test, the more you will be able to identify the critical elements of your design that will lead you to changes in the next iteration of your product. Some of the things you should think about are:

- What do you hope to learn from these tests? Consider the state of your current design, which features are most critical to test at this stage, and what users will really want to do with your system.

- What real-world tasks parallel your goals for the system? Evaluate the kinds of requests your users will have for an interactive supermarket guide.

- Where will you hold the tests? Can you find a location at a local supermarket, or will you simulate a supermarket environment somewhere else?

- How long will you schedule for each test session?

- How many sessions will you conduct altogether?

- Who will conduct the sessions?

- How will you record the sessions?

Method 2: Selecting Test Subjects

Qualifying and recruiting participants for your usability tests (or other user studies).

The people you find to act as potential users for your system are as important as the structure and content of the tests themselves. Typically, "just anyone" will not do as a test subject (unless your user population is made up of many "just anyone's"). The more closely test participants resemble the people that you expect to use your system, the more valuable will be the results.

Identify the target users

In order to find test participants who closely resemble your target users, you must first have a solid understanding of who those users are. Think about factors such as demographics (age, gender, race, and so forth) and user computer experience. While these factors are not always important for every user test you conduct, often they will help you describe the type of person you are expecting to use your system.

Identifying your ideal user type is not always straightforward. There might be times when you don't know exactly who will use your system. In cases like these, you might want to bring in a variety of participants to help you establish who the system is for. In other cases, you might have a clear idea of who will use the system, but for some reason you will not be able to find such people to act as participants in your tests. At these times, the best you can do is to find people who resemble your target users as closely as possible. You will want to take into account the differences in your intended and actual test participants, both in designing your user tests and evaluating the results.

Decide how many participants you need

Think about how many subjects you want to test. You might have difficulty finding as many people as you want to include in the test. If this is the case, use as many "real" representatives as you can find, and fill in the remainder with people who resemble the target users as closely as possible. Better to have the numbers necessary to achieve reasonable conclusions than have just a few people use your system.

You will have to be sensitive to the differences between your more representative users and those who are filling the gaps. Be sure to take advantage of the representative users while you have them by conducting post-test interviews or asking them to complete questionnaires to confirm findings. Ask your "filler" participants to imagine that they are the target users with similar goals; having them roleplay might help you attain more representative results.

Determine the motivation for the participants

Consider how you will motivate subjects to participate in your tests. These people are spending their time to give you valuable information about your system. Depending on who your participants are and the effort they must expend to be a part of your test sessions, you should compensate them accordingly. Willing users (such as friends and family, or graduate students recruited from a local university) might be happy with a complimentary tee-shirt or other token. Food and beverages are also a nice way to reward people for their time.

Participants recruited from other sources, such as some of those noted in the following section, might require more substantial compensation, either in the form of financial remuneration or complimentary versions of your software. Compensating users can be somewhat of an expense, so plan ahead to be sure you can cover your needs for objective and impartial test participants.

Finding the participants

Finding people to participate is sometimes the most daunting task in organizing and carrying out your user test. While you might have a good idea of the kind of people you want, you might not know where to find them. Here are some suggestions:

- Post notices on bulletin boards at local universities or other likely places. Interested people can contact you.

- Place an advertisement in the local paper.

- Ask friends and family to participate. It is a low-cost approach (and the safest for potential confidentiality conflicts), but be aware that they might not give you truly unbiased and critical feedback.

- Use a temporary agency.

- Contact marketing research firms. Sometimes they provide services for locating target users.

Clearly, your compensation budget might come into play here, since these different resources will have varying related fees. You might have to modify the qualifying characteristics of your users somewhat if you do not have the funds to compensate them adequately. In any case, do the best you can to find representative users.

Scheduling the tests

It takes a significant amount of time to recruit and schedule your participants. You should allow a minimum of a week, sometimes four weeks or more, for the process. Don't underestimate the amount of time you will need to accomplish all of these aspects of engaging test participants:

- Contact the potential participants.

- Establish that they are appropriate users.

- Schedule a mutually-convenient test time.

- Send a reminder of the scheduled test session.

- Provide some form of compensation.

- Follow up after the test, if necessary.

You might want to consider delegating some of these tasks, especially the scheduling of participants, to someone with administrative responsibilities who can be reached easily by phone. While it might take you time to plan the participation of your subjects, being organized during scheduling will help ensure smooth-running test sessions and help you get the most from your user tests.

The importance of selecting test subjects

Devoting some energy to qualifying and recruiting your test participants is critical to the success of your user tests because:

Results are only as accurate as your subjects.

If your test participants are not really representative of the people who will use your target software, then the results they present might not be either. In order to truly learn how to improve your system, ask people to participate who will be using it. These kinds of subjects will tell you what you need to know.

They can help you understand your audience.

Sometimes in the design phase of software development, we role-play our users to identify an appropriate creative design. In doing so, we might lose touch with the users themselves and get caught up in the elements of the design. Bringing in test subjects who are your target users—or who represent them well—can help you get back in touch with your audience.

You want people who are motivated, not just anyone.

The right test participants will be motivated to use your software to accomplish tasks, not simply for the purpose of the test session. These users will be able to evaluate the software in light of its actual purpose, not just for the superficial aspects that seem important at test time.

They can be helpful in influencing the design team.

Appropriate test subjects can also help sway the design team to accept the feedback from your user tests. If the design team believes your test participants to be representative of the people who will actually use the system, the team will be more likely to take their comments and criticisms to heart.

They can help you make design decisions and a better product.

Ultimately, your usability tests are what help lead you to a better design and thus a better product. Your test participants will have suggestions and feedback that can help influence your design decisions. In a way, they will act as co-designers on your product. Take their input seriously and heed their suggestions—they are your "expert" users!

Steps for selecting test subjects

1. Make a profile of your system's target users.

2. Decide how many subjects will be necessary for your test. The number of subjects tested will depend on available time and on how statistically accurate you want your results to be. Test enough subjects to eliminate bias from your test results. Account for "no shows" at test time.

3. Decide what kind of compensation you will offer participants. Your budget might affect the types of users you are able to recruit.

4. Identify any confidentiality or security limitations that might apply to your participants.

5. Determine if you will be able to find participants who precisely fit the profile, or if you will have to compromise in some way. If you are compromising, anticipate how this might affect your test or any follow-up interview questions.

6. Plan how you will recruit test subjects. Will you call them directly (if you know who they are), ask colleagues to recruit friends and family, recruit participants from among people you know, or have an agency do the recruiting for you?

7. Contact your participants and be willing to adjust your testing schedule to accommodate their schedules, if necessary. Inform participants that you are counting on their support, in order to avoid no-shows.

Hints/suggestions

Schedule more participants than you think you will actually need. No-shows are, unfortunately, a common occurrence. It can't hurt to have extra sessions, but having too few might not provide representative data.

Think about who your test participants might be from day one of your design, not simply when you want to conduct usability tests. You can then be on the alert for appropriate people and line them up well ahead of time.

Keep a list of potential test participants—people who have expressed interest in being a part of your user tests. If you cannot use some people you have contacted for one test, or if they seem more appropriate for a product down the pipeline, ask them if you might contact them at a later time. This will help save scheduling time in the future.

You might need to travel to find your appropriate users, particularly if you are developing software that serves a niche market that doesn't happen to be in your area. Plan ahead if travel budgeting is an issue.

Exercise task

Think about the test subjects for your supermarket guide usability tests. If you will be able to actually conduct user tests, then go ahead and plan for your subjects and schedule them for the tests. Remember to ask yourself the following questions:

- What qualifications are you looking for in your test participants? Will you want people in a range of ages and socioeconomic standings? Are the people you are thinking about representative of your target users?

- How you will recruit subjects? Where will you find people who meet your criteria? Might you want help from others in locating or engaging these people?

- If you schedule your participants for testing slots, what times will be best for them? Remember to identify a number of alternative time slots so people have some flexibility in choosing—they are doing you a favor by attending, so make it convenient for them.

- How will you compensate these people? Can you provide something that will be appreciated by everyone (such as cash), or will you have to be more creative and individual in your compensation plan due to budget or other constraints?

Method 3: Conducting a User Test

Objectively gathering information about the usability and functionality of a system.

If planning your user tests is the critical aspect of usability testing, then conducting the tests themselves is to enjoy the fruits of your labor. During the user tests, you will observe people using the system to accomplish real tasks, listen to the questions they have about the software, understand what users find straightforward and what they have difficulties with, and in general see your product in action. You will find that test participants have little trouble with some features but serious problems with others that you hadn't anticipated they would. Conducting a user test can be a very telling experience.

Learn from multiple users

When you conduct your user tests, you will gather data about comparative usage among many users. Watching multiple users try to accomplish the same tasks will quickly show you which features users seem to grasp and which are problematic. If one user after another has a problem with something, that is a sign that you will probably have to change that feature. Likewise, if one user has a problem but others seem not to have similar problems, then that problem very likely is not as critical. Depending on the nature of the problem and the user who experienced it, the feature might not need to be changed at all. Comparing one user's performance to that of all other participants will help you understand which findings are the most relevant.

Record the sessions

During the user tests, you should record what transpires to provide documentation of the critical successes and failures of your system. You can make the most of your test sessions if you encourage users to tell you all that they are thinking during the course of the test. This procedure is called "thinking aloud." It is an effective way of encouraging your participants to tell you what they are thinking when something isn't clear, or to explain why they took a particular action.

You have the opportunity to direct users somewhat by asking them questions, but you should be careful not to reveal too much about the system or ask questions that give away what you are trying to get them to do. Questions should focus on getting participants to think aloud when they are otherwise quiet. And whatever you do, refrain from answering participants' questions, particularly if your answers reveal exactly the type of information you are trying to learn from them. For example, suppose a user asks you, "What does this button do?" Instead of answering directly, turn it around by asking the user, "What do you think it does?" You will learn much more about how your system is working and your users' expectations if you prompt users to answer their own questions. It might take a little longer, but the results are well worth it. Also remember that by asking users numerous questions, you prompt them to share their ideas and design recommendations for improving your system.

Post-test interviews and questionnaires

As a final part of your testing sessions, you might choose to interview users, or discuss various issues either directly or indirectly relating to their performance during the test. If so, then you should prepare an interview form and schedule some time at the end of the test to complete this interview.

Another useful approach is to have participants complete an evaluative questionnaire when they are done with the test. Having them write their thoughts or opinions down on paper without you personally interviewing them might allow them to be more objective. You might want to use a Likert scale to permit users to respond to questions with a scaled evaluation. For example, you could use a scale of 1-to-5 or 1-to-10, where 1 represents "Strongly Agree" and 5 (or 10) represents "Strongly Disagree." Numeric responses on the questionnaire gives you a definitive means of evaluation or comparison.

Example of conducting a user test

Figure 7.3 A user test in progress. In this video frame, the test participant sits at the computer while the test conductor sits to the side observing the events of the test. This user test took place in a typical office cubicle, which is where the test designer predicts the developing application would be used. The test conductor takes notes during the test, but video tapes the entire session to be sure not to miss anything.

During the test

Make the most of your testing sessions. Pay attention to all the major activities: watch what your users do; listen to the questions they ask or observations they make; record critical findings on video tape (record the entire session, if you can); gather additional information through spontaneous (but not leading) questions, final interviews, or questionnaires. Not all sessions will require you to complete all of these activities, or even allow you time to do so. But don't expect to simply sit back and take it easy during your test sessions. Your mind should be constantly working to analyze results on the spot so you can clarify points with your participants while you have them there.

The importance of conducting a user test

Since usability testing is the most widely practiced user-centered design technique, its advantages are fairly well understood. Usability tests are important because they let you:

Understand where the system works and where it doesn't.

Watching objective test participants use your system will clearly indicate what works and what doesn't. There will be no more need for heated design discussion or arguments about which approach will work best with your users. Seeing users accomplish tasks or not will set you or your colleagues straight about what is right for your software.

Experience first hand what real users think.

It is one thing to be told that users like or dislike a certain feature. This is almost like having a design argument where one team member backs up his side with his perceptions of users and another team member similarly backs up her argument. There is no substitute, however, for experiencing first hand what users really do with—and think about—your system. Videotaping user test sessions can be important because your video clips allow you to share the first-hand experience with others who were not present during the test.

Generate data to improve the user interface.

The best reason to conduct user tests is to help you gather data that will help you make your system better. This is the purpose of conducting user tests—to let your participants lead you to your design problems and potential solutions. While it's nice when your users tell you that they like your system, the more important information you gather from them concerns where the system needs improvement and why.

Steps for conducting a user test

1. Greet users and give a general description of the test. Don't provide detailed instructions about how to perform the tasks.

2. Inform users that they can stop at any time.

3. Talk about and demonstrate any equipment in the room.

4. Encourage users to think aloud (explain this if necessary).

5. Explain that you will not provide help during the test. Encourage users to ask any questions that occur, and explain that you will answer any unresolved questions at the end of the test.

6. Describe the tasks and give the users written instructions, if appropriate.

7. Ask if there are any questions before you start.

8. Conduct the test. Allow users to progress at their own pace.

9. Conclude the observation. Discuss any responses that you want explained in more detail. Conduct an interview or have the user complete a questionnaire if you have this planned. Answer any remaining questions, and tell what you were trying to accomplish, if users are interested.

Hints/suggestions

- Give written instructions if that will help the user to feel more comfortable with the task. Written instructions are particularly useful when the task requires more than one step, and you don't want the user to rely on having to ask you (which might be inhibiting). Don't give written instructions if you think the written form will somehow influence the results of the test.

- Remember not to tell the user too much about the purpose of your test, either before it begins or during it. Greet the user with a simple explanation, such as, "We are testing a system for making airline reservations," rather than a longer description of the system and its many features.

- When you videotape your sessions, obtain a written release for the videotaping, especially if your participants are not employees of your company (or the company for whom you are conducting the test). This can take care of confidentiality agreements when you are showing sensitive information, as well as clear you from any legal situations that might occur down the road if you use the video clip of that user in a presentation or demonstration.

- Write down the steps for conducting the user test and take the list with you to each testing session. Reading the steps from a piece of paper will help you to remember them and free you to focus on other significant information.

Exercise task

Carry out the user tests you designed with the users you identified in the two preceding exercises. Remember to:

- Greet users and make them feel comfortable without revealing too much about your test.

- Observe and listen during each session without interruption. You will have time later to clarify issues or ask questions.

- During the session, carefully follow user responses so that you can ask any clarifying questions later.

- Prompt users to think aloud; prompt repeatedly with "what" rather than with "why" questions, if necessary, even though that might feel awkward. Remember, you are conducting these tests to find out what users think. When users show some doubt or hesitation, ask them to articulate their thoughts.

- Let participants follow an unplanned task path if you think it will reveal additional information about your system. If you think it won't, however, and you are short on time, steer them back on the planned course.

Method 4: Analyzing Test Results

Evaluating data gathered from user tests to identify elements that will help to improve the user interface.

When your user tests are complete, your work is not yet done; in some ways, it has only just begun. Now that you have gathered the data which can critically change your design for the better, you must interpret the information to make the most of it. Some of your findings will provide clear indications about where to make changes, and might even include information about the changes themselves. However, other findings will be more elusive, and you will have to spend adequate time sorting through them, especially those where the results from one participant conflict with those of another.

Compare goals and results

Before you form conclusions about the overall findings, check your results against the goals of the test. Go back to your list of goals and remind yourself of what you were trying to learn. Then when you review your records of the test sessions, keep these points in mind. Since you presumably structured the test tasks to accomplish these goals, you should have findings that provide such information. At this point of findings analysis, you don't yet want to think about how to change your design. Simply assess your findings—design alternatives will come later.

Look for patterns in the results

Look for patterns of usage among multiple users. If one user after another stumbles over the same feature, then chances are that it is a significant problem. Patterns of usage need not mean that all participants make exactly the same mistakes—results that might seem superficially different can actually provide support for the same finding. An example of this is when one participant selects the wrong icon to perform a task and another wrongly chooses a menu command to perform that same function. Chances are that you do not need to change the icon and menu; rather, you probably need to make more prominent the feature that accomplishes that task.

Review test records

It is a good idea to review recordings (either audio or video) to find additional data or to verify assumed findings. Watching or listening to your recordings can take large amounts of time, but keep in mind that these tapes will help you remember exactly what went on during the tests. After all, this is the primary reason you made the recordings. If you are short on time, be subjective about which tapes you review—choose the ones that you believe contain controversial data or are packed with the most information. If you can, share the viewing and analyzing of the tapes with others on your design team.

Document your findings

Videotape or write down your findings. If you follow your original test goals, you will probably be able to categorize findings in the same way. You might also find that other categories become evident through the results of your test. Organizing your findings into categories will not only help you structure your results, it can make the findings clearer to others who might read them. When you document your findings, consider including examples or quotes directly from the test sessions. First-hand examples will help your audience visualize what happened during the tests and lend support to your assessment.

Timing of the analysis

The best time to analyze test results is just after you have completed a user test because the responses and behaviors of users will still be fresh in your mind. However, once you have completed the early analysis of your user tests, don't throw out your test notes. You might find that you want to reanalyze your findings later in your design process, particularly if further tests show conflicting results. Referring to your notes to review the results of earlier tests might help shed new light on a finding.

The importance of analyzing test results

Your user test findings will lead you to the changes that will make your design more responsive to the needs and expectations of your users. Taking the time to critically analyze your test results is important because it can help you to:

Gather information on system usability and functionality.

Seeing where your users have problems or where operations run smoothly gives you the information you need about how usable your system is. After just a few user testing sessions, you will have a fairly basic understanding of the general usability of your software, but careful analysis of the test session data can help you see just what works and what doesn't. You will also answer questions about the features themselves, such as: Do users find them appropriate? Do users take advantage of them? These are the kinds of questions you will ask yourself in determining if the current functionality is appropriate for supporting your users in completing their tasks.

Check actual findings against expectations.

When you create the goals for your user tests and generate tasks to attain those goals, you probably set expectations about what you think the system is capable of and what users' responses will be. Reviewing the results of your test sessions will help you to check those expectations against what really happens when people sit down with your system. Analyzing the findings will not only help you make alternative design decisions, it will prepare you for how your software might be received in the real world by its actual users.

Discover ideas that improve the system.

Test participants, when they are supportive of your system and cooperative in terms of the testing situation, can be incredible allies in the design of your software. They will give you suggestions for better design alternatives, or compare your system to others that approach the same tasks in alternative ways. They will almost always introduce ideas that you had not considered but that could enhance or improve your software. Sometimes you will not even remember that your participants had such strong ideas, but in reviewing the test data you will come across statements such as these. Taking the time to go back over your notes or video recordings can help you discover these excellent ideas.

Identify any missing features.

In addition to giving you ideas about how to change features that you have in your system, your test participants can be great at identifying features that you overlooked. Often they will say, "This is nice, but what I really expected or wanted was a system that does that." You might have considered such a feature and purposely omitted it, or you might not have even thought about it. Whatever the case, if your users are telling you that this feature is something they want in your system, then you should seriously consider including it.

```
              Faculty Reserves Project
              Usability Test Findings

                 GENERAL FINDINGS

Overall, participants seemed to find the system
relatively straightforward to use and were able to
complete all tasks.  Most of the participants
preferred this system to the existing process for
placing items on reserve.  Comments included that
they thought the on-line system was "infinitely more
delightful" or "far better" since it saves walking
to the library.  One participant said "to think this
is going to be possible is wonderful", and another
noted that by using this system she would be more
likely to get reserves in promptly.  The one user
who said the system wasn't really necessary noted
that he typically places items on reserves about
once a year, so it would be more trouble for him to
learn a new process than to continue with the
existing process.

Both faculty and administrative users thought the
system would make it easier for faculty to place
items on reserves themselves, and that they would
recommend to their colleagues and faculty members
that they use the system. A couple of administrative
participants thought that some faculty members
wouldn't use it and they would have to continue to
enter reserves for them, but they noted that these
were the kind of faculty members who had their
administrators do this kind of work for them in any
case.
```

Figure 7.4 User test findings. This document presents general findings from usability tests at Stanford University to evaluate a prototype system for using on-line services to place items on reserves at campus libraries. The general findings section sum-

One participant did make the point that while she really liked this system, there were some perceived advantages to the current paper-based method, such as she had the impression that she could take her time with the paper approach and not have to worry about being able to support the application on her minimally configured computer. She did say, however, that if the on-line system offered obvious advantages, such as the ability to copy and paste from Socrates, then she would definitely prefer the electronic system.

A couple of participants expressed concern that they thought users might not be Mac-literate, and that we might want to make specific help available for non-Mac users. This help might include an introduction to pop-up menus, or to clicking in a field to type there. One participant wanted to see the system on the PC instead of a Mac, since it was his belief that few faculty members had or used Macs. We need to know who our users are (and specifically if we really do have to worry about non-Mac users) before we make any such changes.

marizes users' reactions to the overall system and highlights key details. Using quotes from or describing the reactions of individual users can present what actually went on during the tests to help explain the findings.

Steps for analyzing test results

1. Review any notes you took during the test. Try to remember what you were thinking as the sessions were going on.

2. Review recordings of the test.

3. Make a list of any trends in user behavior or other important findings. Try not to solve any problems here—just list findings. Back up your claim with information about where the problem occurred.

4. List positive findings as well as negative ones.

5. Group findings according to logical categories. You might be able to use categories corresponding to your goals from your test design. If those categories don't fit, don't feel obligated to use them.

6. Within categories, order findings from "most important" to "least important."

Hints/suggestions

-   Realize that analyzing the results of each test session might be a time-consuming task. You might need to review notes more than once, checking to see if they match the written findings you are generating.

-   Be careful not to make assumptions too early and force results to match your expectations or user responses. Be objective in analyzing your results and you will produce much more realistic findings.

-   As you review test session notes, write down direct quotes when they are available and succinctly summarize the problems you are trying to identify. Using direct quotes from test

participants can be a powerful communication device in later
reports or presentations.

- You might want to catalog video or audio tapes to help you
locate critical clips later, particularly if you plan to edit segments of the tape for documentation or presentation purposes.
Or perhaps you can enlist someone else to catalog them for
you. (To catalog a tape, view it in its entirety and make a
detailed record of what is covered; note important discussions
or events and the elapsed time at which they occur.)

Exercise task

Analyze the results of your user tests and generate a document listing the
findings. Following the steps above, categorize the findings—either according to your original test goals, if this makes sense, or to system functionality, or some other appropriate structure. Prioritize findings within your categories. In generating the findings, think about the following questions:

- What are some of the patterns of behavior you saw from user
to user? Were there any that all users showed?

- What are the findings that only one or two users exhibited?
Why do you think only a small portion of your participants
had such results, and should those results have any bearing
on your further system development?

- Did your participants have any suggestions for missing features? Did they seem to think that any of the included features could be omitted?

- Did you use an organizational structure in your notes? If so,
did it help you to organize your thoughts either during note
taking or when you were assessing the findings?

- Are any of your findings contradictory? How will you resolve
it? (You might need to conduct another user test!)

- If you recorded the sessions, how will you refer to the recordings? What kinds of information did you learn from your recordings that you were unable to gather in your notes?

Method 5: Making Design Recommendations

Generating ideas for redesigning the system based on findings from user studies, user tests, or other evaluation.

Once you have objectively gathered the test results and generated a list of findings, it is time to start thinking about what you have learned and how it can positively influence your design. Rather than simply attacking your software to make changes directly, spend some time determining redesign solutions and assessing those that make the most sense for further development. You are now ready to draw up a list of design recommendations that describe alternatives for system design in response to the problems found by your users in the test sessions.

Identifying the recommendations

Design recommendations are suggestions for how the user interface could be changed to alleviate a problem or better meet user needs. When you make design recommendations, present specific solutions—in fact, be as specific as possible. For instance, if your test participants had problems locating the Quit item in the menu, a vague design recommendation might be, "Change the Quit item in the menu." A clearer, more helpful recommendation would be, "Instead of placing the Quit item in the menu, place a Quit button on the screen in a clearly visible place." Another possible recommendation would be, "Move the Quit item to the top of the menu, and spell it with all capital letters." Each of these more explicit recommendations provides better direction for implementation, and also leaves no room for questioning your intent.

Support recommendations with findings

The recommendations will have even more strength if supported by the findings from your test results analysis. Your findings can provide a clear explanation for the recommendations. Particularly if you will be handing off your design recommendations to someone else to implement the changes, it is important to explain the the users' actions that led you to your recommendation. Even if you will be using the recommendations to make changes to the software yourself, listing them with test findings will remind you of why you made a decision. This is especially useful if you don't get around to implementing changes until later, when you might forget your reasoning.

Devise alternative recommendations

Another reason that listing your findings along with recommendations can be useful is that if you find that you are constrained by your system from implementing a particular recommendation, you can study your findings to determine another design alternative. This is good reason to devise more than one solution for a design problem, or more than one recommendation for each finding.

Giving alternatives is useful not only for the system implementer at build time, but might also prove helpful later on. If the design recommendation you choose to follow does not alleviate the original problem, you can try an alternative solution. Having another design that addresses the problem will then save you time.

Consider having the alternative solution handy at the user tests, either as a prototype, a storyboard, or even simply a verbal description, to bounce off of users who seem dissatisfied with the implemented solution. More than one design recommendation gives you bargaining power if you are simply delivering test results and recommendations for changes to others who will implement the changes. You can together select the one that makes the most sense based on what you know about users and what they know about the software.

Airline Scheduling Options

Allow for "any time" or "any am/pm time" as a time scheduling choice.

Many users did not care what time their flights departed, or wanted to be able to say "any time in the morning." They tried to do this by leaving the time field blank, but on submitting the request were warned that they were leaving out the time, and thus felt that they had to then enter it. A separate "any time" option would allow the user to say to the system "I intentionally did not specify a time."

Support users being able to specify options such as "Non-stop Flight Preferred," "First Class," "Business Class," and the type of seat preferred (aisle, window).

Many users stressed the importance of these options. If the default is for non-stop flight, this was nowhere communicated to users and needs to be done. Having an explicit option makes this clear.

Lodging Options

Provide additional choices in the popup menu for room type. Include "Single Room", "Two Double Beds", "King Bed", "Suite" and "Other" with a field for entering the "Other" information.

The available room choices seemed inadequate, and users were confused about having to use the remarks field and the popup menu. These were the predominantly suggested choices.

Figure 7.5 A design recommendation document. These excerpts from design recommendations for an on-line travel system illustrate the effectiveness of presenting each recommendation

In the "City where hotel needed" field, provide a
popup menu made up of all previously entered
destinations. Better yet, access the hotel
information from the itinerary-based model
(described above) so that when the lodging screen is
accessed the current destination appears in the city
field.

Many users felt they had already entered the
destination in the schedule screen, and wished the
computer would keep track of the destination for
them.

**Have users specify dates for hotel and car, rather
than total number of nights.**

Many users noted they believed date information
should be given rather than number of nights.
Again, if the itinerary model is followed this will
be straightforward because the dates can default to
the given flight dates. Dates must be able to be
changed, however, in case the user does not want the
hotel for all the nights. With date information,
number of nights becomes irrelevant. Alone, number
of nights information is incomplete if it is less
than the total number of nights from the flight.

backed up by the findings of the tests. Each design recommendation is presented as a clear, affirmative statement of action. The
findings help explain the reason for the given recommendation.

The importance of making design recommendations

After summarizing test findings and presenting user feedback regarding your system, design recommendations are truly the next step in the generation of your software. Making design recommendations is important because it allows you to:

Document a plan of action for further system development.

Design recommendations tell the system implementors what to do next to address problems discovered during user tests. When design recommendations are properly documented and presented, they serve as a prioritized plan of action. Whether you or others implement that plan, it helps to organize future work and make the most of implementation time.

Communicate user test results to the design team.

When you are not the person implementing the changes made apparent by the user tests, you need a clear way to communicate with the implementation team. The process of gathering test findings and generating design recommendations provides you with a straightforward way to express to the implementation team what they must do and why. It won't be your word against theirs, but rather their design against what the people who used it think about it.

Improve the system from the user's point of view.

Ultimately, what design recommendations should address are the changes users have either suggested themselves or indicated were necessary by their interaction with the software and user interface. This means that the recommendations should list ways to improve the system from the user's point of view. Again, the design decisions should not come down to what various members of the design team think to be true, but what users really want and need.

Steps for making design recommendations

1. Using the findings from your analysis of the user test, make at least one design recommendation for each item in the list. Clearly indicate the finding and the associated recommendation.

2. Suggest positive alternatives for change. Saying something like, "The Help icon should be changed" is not as useful as saying, "Change the Help icon to something users recognize to indicate help, such as a question mark."

3. Support your recommendations with results from your findings. Describe the situation in which a problem occurred. Better yet, include audio or video recordings with your design recommendations that clearly indicate user difficulty. Sequential snippets of multiple users having the same problem can be extremely effective.

4. If appropriate, brainstorm with others, using the findings to help generate design recommendations.

5. List more than one recommendation per finding to give implementation alternatives.

Hints/suggestions

- Go back to some of the suggestions users themselves had during the tests. They might have had some very good ideas for changing the design. Look for ideas that were given by more than one user. This is a clear indication that people think a certain problem would be better solved by this alternative.

- Use your findings to get to the root of the problem, so that your design recommendation can address this problem and not a superficial indicator. If users could not find an item on the screen, was it because of its visual design, its location, or that they didn't even know to look for that element? Review what users said when you asked them why they had a problem or what they were thinking. This can help influence the design recommendation you make.

- If you are really having trouble deciding among multiple approaches to a problem, then you might not have gathered enough information during your tests to guide you. If possible, go back to your users and ask for clarification. Or, realize that you might want to test these issues again as quickly as possible to understand the real problem.

- Don't be afraid to be creative here—users don't always tell you everything you need to know. Often they will indicate that something didn't work but won't be sure what would have worked better. Use your design skills to come up with something that addresses the problems exhibited during the tests.

Exercise task

Using the findings from the previous exercise task, generate design recommendations and create an implementation plan for making changes to your system. Write down the findings. After each one, write down a design recommendation or two. As you are documenting your alternatives, ask yourself the following questions:

- What is this finding telling me about the user interface? Is the feature itself wrong, or is it simply the way the feature is displayed or accessed that doesn't seem to be working? What is it about the feature that users don't like? Is there anything about it that they do like?

- Are there patterns of problems that might lead to a large, general recommendation, such as to put all of the functions in the menu into on-screen icons? Sometimes your users will not be able to broadly categorize problems, but you might recognize them when grouping various findings together.

- Did users suggest anything that would make a good design alternative? Did they say something like, "I think this icon should look more like a cash register," or anything else that gives you an idea for an alternative design?

- Are there other people who observed the tests or with whom you have discussed the tests who might have suggestions?

- Did you create a design that allowed most of your users to accomplish most of the tasks? If not, then you might need to go back to the drawing board and revamp—maybe your users weren't who you thought they were!

Chapter 8

Iteration

What Is Iteration?

User interface prototyping and design methods are most effective when they are used in a progressive design fashion. Design iteration allows you to make the best use of the various techniques, incorporating suggestions based on user feedback and employing alternative prototyping methodologies to evolve an improved, fine-tuned system or application. In the user-centered design process, iteration refers to the continuous process of creative user interface design, implementation of the various design stages in some off- or on-line format, and testing the design to obtain critical user feedback.

The informal nature of the individual techniques presented in earlier chapters permits them to be used in combination with other techniques, particularly in an iterative process of designing, building, and testing your software. Not every project falls neatly into a design-build-test loop. Some projects might start with testing, and others involve design-test-build-test sequences. What is important in any of these approaches is to recognize that multiple stages of design allow you to best integrate user input by working out design details at each stage rather than trying to get the whole thing perfect the first time. Iteration is about revising a system design in small steps, exploring the features and functionality of your system at each step, identifying what might be wrong with your system, and solving the most critical problems first rather than all the problems at once.

Plan for iteration

In planning your design process, be aware of the value of this revisionary process and anticipate at least two or three iterations so that you can truly put the user interface development techniques to work. In each stage of the iteration, build a prototype that showcases the functionality or general interaction principles you are trying to explore. Don't worry about getting every detail right, but do choose off- or on-line prototyping techniques that enable you to test the principles you want. Then design user studies or tests to examine those principles. Note that the reference to test in the design-build-test sequence encompasses both user tests and more informal studies as appropriate. Evaluate your test results, and, in the next stage of iteration, try to resolve the problems you encountered. If necessary, use the next iterative step to introduce additional functions or features. Typically, early stages will explore broad issues, and later iterations will refine the interface and examine features and functions in more detail.

A cyclical process of development

Design iteration lends itself to a cyclical process of development. Normally, each iteration includes some design, implementation, and testing, even if in reduced or refined forms. The process is cyclical primarily because there seems to be no obvious ending point. Usually you do not want to end with testing because you want to incorporate your test results into the next design iteration. You also do not want to end with design, since you want to be sure that your design changes are incorporated in the implementation of your application or system.

The "end" of the process will most likely be implementation, when you have incorporated changes from the last user session into a new design and then bring the design to working order. Ending with implementation is, of course, not ideal because it does not provide an opportunity to obtain feedback from another round of user tests. However, if there have been enough iteration cycles, then the problems you might encounter should be minimal.

You have to end sometime. Occasionally, when the results of testing show that users are overwhelmingly pleased with the system, you might end there. Users, however, can almost always find something unsettling about your system, and it is nearly impossible to have identified problems through user testing and then not incorporate them in your work—even severely time-constrained schedules seem to find room for such updates. Therefore, you will usually end with a (potentially very short) implementation step.

Ideally, you should include as many iterations as necessary to refine the design until you are satisfied. This way, you can let the design's progress dictate whether more user feedback is needed. In the real world, however, we are often limited by time or other resources. When your development constraints are known, plan at least two iterations, even if short and limited in scope. Having the opportunity to bring users in to see your design, get feedback, and revise the design will result in a more usable and attractive user interface and system.

Integrate user test results

The most compelling reason to apply an iterative design approach is to be able to integrate the findings from the user studies and tests into your designs recommendations. Clearly, if you do not plan to iterate your design, you shouldn't bother to conduct tests, since you won't be able to incorporate any of the user feedback.

Other reasons for iterative design

There are other reasons to follow an iterative design process, as well.

- You might be able to take advantage of different resources available to you in various phases of the design. This is particularly helpful if not all of your staff is continuously available, or if you have a limited research and design budget.

- It allows you to focus on subsets of the user interface, concentrating on them individually instead of having to always think about the whole picture.

- It permits you to improve your design with each successive effort. This is, perhaps, the most important reason for iterative design. You will see evidence of the improvements through users' responses to your evolving interface, and feel secure that you are building a system that meets users' needs. Iterative design will support your creative effort and lead you to develop usable, dependable software.

The Advantages of Iteration

Iteration in the design process is advantageous in many ways. When applied successfully, iterative design can:

Incrementally build the best system possible.

Approaching your design in smaller, well-focused stages will almost always lead you to a better design. Breaking down the design process into a series of steps will allow you to focus on a smaller set of issues and problems, introducing only the features or functions that you intend to explore at that stage. You can design a prototype that showcases those few concepts, then conduct user tests aimed at specifically addressing those concepts. In increments, you will be building up to a fine-tuned, user-sensitive interface.

Support stages of development and user feedback.

User feedback plays a significant role in the software development process. Acknowledging that you will conduct some period of creative design and then present your work in an intermediate stage to potential users is critical in supporting user input. Planning for design iteration writes user participation directly into your schedule and says you will put your design on hold until potential users have given the go-ahead. Iterative design makes user-centered design possible.

Integrate the work of designers, user specialists, and programmers.

Having different stages of design that play different roles in the overall development process permits you to integrate smoothly the roles of the various interdisciplinarians on your design team. Each expert can lead that stage of the iteration that best utilizes his or her skills—the designers can be responsible for design sessions, user specialists for involving users and obtaining feedback, and programmers (or others responsible for implementation) for getting the whole thing to actually work. Each skill is important in its own right. All team members can participate in each stage, but having skilled individuals responsible for corresponding segments will help everyone work together as a team and make the best use of their talents.

Help you concentrate on system development without fear of failure.

Knowing that your design follows an iterative process will help you concentrate on the issues or problems you want to address in the current design. Rather than trying to get everything perfect at every stage, you can focus on the issues that are most important in the current stage. Once you complete this phase of design and obtain user feedback, you can concentrate on the next potential development area—there's always the next cycle of iteration if something goes wrong with your current design. This knowledge will help you relax and tackle the issues or problems at hand.

Build robust, successful systems.

Ideally, what you want to do is design and build great software. Iterative design will support this end by allowing you to incorporate all of the user-centered techniques (or as many as make sense for your design) and build software that addresses user needs. These are the systems and applications that make the most robust and successful software. Rather than hope to get lucky with a design, you can focus your efforts on what your users are telling you they want this system to be and do. Think of this as applied creative design, and as a process that will almost always lead you to successful software.

How to Design and Perform Iteration

Iteration is not as simple as following a sequence of processes numerous times. While you will often fall into a design-build-test cycle, you might not always start with the design stage, or your stages might not always follow one another in the same order. Knowing where to start and where to end your design is critical in user-centered design iteration.

Spend time outlining and planning

Previous chapters present reasons and methods for planning and scheduling various stages of prototyping. Iteration is the culmination of all of these planning and scheduling efforts. Planning to include iteration in your design process takes a little time up front, but unless such planning is done at the beginning of the project, it is almost impossible to incorporate later.

Spend the time necessary at the beginning of your development process to understand your design problem and how many iterations might be necessary. Plan to bring users in at least twice to help evaluate your progress. Understand when it makes the most sense for users to be brought in, and what types of prototyping can be accomplished in the time you have. If you are fortunate enough to have an open-ended development schedule, plan at least your first two iteration cycles to help put some structure in your design process. Determine when users might be available and set time limits around each iteration to aid you in identifying appropriate prototyping methodologies and goals. Don't underestimate the value of the planning time necessary to structure a successful iterative design process.

Build flexible component-based systems

Component-based or object-oriented systems are touted more and more in all kinds of software development processes. Such approaches to software design are equally valuable in user interface development, particularly for on-line prototypes implemented in code. Component-based systems are adaptable to change, and change is a critical characteristic of evolving iterative designs. Your design should be able to adapt readily to accommodate design changes or user feedback; it can prove frustrating if software limitations prevent this. Object-oriented systems do not ensure that all changes can be made as desired, but in most cases they make the task significantly easier. Programs that are hacked together will probably be more difficult to change later.

Work closely with all team members

Understand the skills of the members of the design team and those stages of iterative design for which they are best qualified. Work together to make the most of your development process. An advantage of iterative design is that it puts many different skills to use.

While complete stages of development must happen in succession, some work can probably go on simultaneously in more than one stage. You will not only make the most of your design team, but also of your total available time. However, don't pigeonhole people, relegating them to particular roles. Encourage input from all team members at all stages of development. You will then be able to incorporate the ideas of others, and continually improve on the design.

Don't become attached to implementation details

For iterative design to be successful, the whole design must be considered a work in progress. Keep an open mind about implementation so that if user feedback shows the need for change, anything is expendable. Too often developers become attached to certain features or interactive methods in the user interface, or to some concise or novel algorithm used to implement the design. In evaluating your designs, remember that the software is only as useful as it is usable—if users don't like or need the features you are sure are critical to your design, or say something that refutes your need for that brilliant algorithm, be willing to let it go. To best accomplish iteration, you must be free to make requested design changes.

Understand the nature of your design

Thinking about the type of product you are developing can help you to understand how many iterations might be needed to appropriately refine the design. If you believe your design to be truly innovative and that it introduces new functionality or methods of interaction, then chances are it will demand a higher number of iterations than a design that relies more heavily on known approaches or standards.

The higher the risk you will take with your software, the more you should plan to involve users. Allocate time for alternative design development in case user feedback indicates significant problems in your general approach. On the other hand, applying known user interface techniques, such as those specified in standards, presents appreciably lower risk to your interface development process and might therefore require less user feedback to help you evaluate it.

Plan for each iteration stage

With each iteration, identify what must be changed before revising your prototype. As at the beginning of the project, evaluate what you know about the design and how you want it to progress. Your initial plan is the starting point; update it according to what you have learned in the most recent design or user feedback session. Prioritize activities according to a schedule. Understand what you want to accomplish in the next stage, how you might next involve users, and what you will leave for a later design stage. In doing so, you will have a record of your plans and might save significant time later.

Verify design changes

Transfer what you have learned from one design stage to the next. Keep track of the design changes you make as a result of feedback from user tests, and be sure to retest those changes in your next iteration. Simply making design changes in response to user feedback is not enough—they might be worthless unless users indicate problems have been alleviated in successive tests. This is the whole reason for iteration: to refine your design so it best meets user needs. Make the most of iteration by checking your design changes as your design progresses.

Method 1: Deciding on Next Steps

To identify what to do next in your prototyping cycle, which typically takes place after a user test has been conducted and before the next development phase begins.

At some point in each design iteration, the design reaches the end of its potential and it is time to move on to the next iteration. Usually, this happens after a series of user tests, when you have feedback that you want to incorporate in a new version of the design. A typical iterating pattern is made up of design-build-test sequences, where each sequence is a single iteration.

```
   Home Library System
   Prioritized Action List

1. Resolve layout/design problems
     • Adjust use of screen space in main screen -
       center card catalog, make desk space less
       prominent
     • Affordances for all buttons (so users know
       what is active)
     • Make all similar button locations consistent
       throughout, particularly for return to main
       screen and general navigation

2. Redesign card catalog interface
     • Change to straight alpha list (one drawer
       each A - Z)
     • Allow "thumb" to section, as in a dictionary
     • Support customized markers
     • Store marker in an alternate drawer

3. Fix error notification and dialog problems
     • Set error sound to system beep
     • Error notification for selection of
       non-active book on main screen
     • Check dialog wordings

4. Provide command key interface
     • Command key equivalents for navigation:
       forward, back, main
     • Hints card with command keys

5. Help
     • General interface and availability
     • Context-sensitivity to respond to specific
       needs
```

Figure 8.1 Prioritized list of action from usability test findings. Once design recommendations have been identified, action items can be generated and prioritized. The most important actions are listed first to be implemented first, and less important items are at the end of the list. This list of actions acts as a plan for next steps in the design process, and can be followed much as a do-to list.

Analyze the situation

The first task in moving to the next iteration is to decide what you will do in that stage of design. This decision facilitates the transition from one iteration to the next and is, in fact, a vital part of iterative user interface design.

Between design stages, take the time to analyze the situation. Assessing your most recent iteration as well as the next can help make the most of your time and resources. Think about what you were trying to accomplish in the last cycle—what goals did you set for the user testing? Even earlier, what was the basis of your design?

If this iteration ended with user testing, examine what your users told you or showed you. If you made recommendations based on the findings from the user tests, evaluate which make the most sense to address in your next iteration. Consider how to revise your goals for the next phase based on what you now know about your most recent design. Set goals for the next stage if you did not have any in particular for the last phase. Understand what you hope to achieve in the next design cycle, and think about how you will meet your goals.

A useful way to check your progress and make sure your design is on track is to set development goals and evaluate them at the end of a design stage. At the end of an iteration, review the progress of the design. Are you meeting original goals or expectations? Do users agree that you met those goals (or even that those goals were important)? Use the results of your user tests to help evaluate goals. What did you learn from the testing that you didn't expect to? More important, consider how this information might affect your design—changes you could make to functionality or features, or presentation of interactive methods. Assess the changes you might propose and how they might affect your development schedule. What will you be able to accomplish in the next round if you are time-constrained? If you don't have external constraints, determine how long it might take you to accomplish all that you hope to.

Team meetings to discuss progress

Take the time between iterations to meet as a team and talk about next steps. You don't have to devote much time to this—a few hours will suffice. Simply provide an opportunity for the team to get together, discuss what you have learned, and share ideas about the design direction. This will set the foundation for the next phase of design. Meeting as a team will offer everyone a chance to express his or her individual concerns at this early point, before the next design is undertaken. Supporting teamwork can prove especially useful to the overall design process.

Devoting time to deciding your next steps is a way to assess what you have achieved up to now in your design. It provides an opportunity to reassess your development goals. Deciding your next steps allows you to carefully analyze the results of any user tests your might have just conducted. It gives you an opportunity to gather input from all team members before you dive in and make changes. It helps you make the most of time and resources. Taking the time to decide what to do supports a multiple-stage development cycle in many ways and is critical to successful user interface design.

The importance of deciding on next steps

Planning what you will do next before simply moving to the next development phase is vital to your design's success for a number of reasons:

It gives you an opportunity to assess current and progressing work.

Even in a short time, you can surmise the critical findings from your most recent phase of development and begin to plan for the next phase. Stopping to ask yourself what the goals are of your design, especially those in terms of your users, can help avoid simply executing the design because it's there, or choosing a development path arbitrarily. Understanding what you have done so far with your design, what you have learned from your most recent tests can help lead to a usable design.

Help make the most of time and resources.

While it might seem that planning what to do next is a drain on available time, in the long run it will almost always save you time that would be wasted by going down the wrong development path. Think about what a waste of time it would be to spend weeks on a development effort that must be discarded later. The nominal time you spend in assessing your work thus far and planning the upcoming stage will be worth the effort. Make the most of available resources by gathering input from the entire design team about what you have accomplished and what to do next. Short checkpoints improve the overall quality of the design.

Provide structure for your design process.

Planning efforts often lend themselves to structuring your development process. While identifying a structure or plan of action requires some critical analysis, it will set guidelines for future design work and make your job easier later on. Even if your plan changes, having one as a reference point will help you check your progress. If you record the plan, it will be even easier to track. Months or even years later, you might want to refer to this stage of design and understand why you interpreted your findings the way you did. Creating this record will take little time now, and might provide important information later.

Steps for deciding next steps

1. Gather findings from your most recent usability tests, or any other information reflecting the state of your system (such as results of an evaluation or design session).

2. If recommendations addressing those findings are not available, generate at least one recommendation for each finding you have. Spell out what can be done to address a problem or development issue.

3. Assess all the recommendations together. Do any preclude others? Can some be grouped together? Do any have implications for completing others?

4. Prioritize the list of actions you will take to address the problems. Base them on your recommendations, but adapt them to the actual situation and constraints.

5. Identify which of these actions you can take in the next development stage according to your time and resources. Follow the priority order when possible, but consider omitting certain actions if it means you can accomplish more with others.

6. Think about what your end product will be. Will you build another prototype for a successive series of user tests? Will the prototype be on- or off-line, and which methodologies make the most sense?

7. Keep a list of the actions that you could not—or chose not—to address. You might be able to use this list in later development.

Hints/suggestions

- Don't try to do everything. Even when you are not restricted by time or budget, it will rarely make sense to implement every potential change identified in testing or that is left over from an earlier design stage. Think about all of the possibilities together, understand how they interrelate, and choose the ones that solve the most problems.

- Realize that the end product of this iteration need not be the same as the end product for the stage before it or after it. Just because your last design was on-line does not mean you cannot now have an off-line prototype, particularly if user tests have shown you need to re-evaluate your overall solution. A user study might even be needed at advanced stages of the design. While you should be working toward a final software revision, you need not necessarily do so by moving linearly from off- to on-line. If it makes sense to develop a rougher prototype at any stage of the design, by all means do so.

- Consider alternative recommendations and how they affect your design schedule, especially when you are constrained by time or cost factors. The purpose of identifying multiple design recommendations is that one might make more sense than another when it comes time for implementation. Iteration is the time when you commit to the implementation—evaluate the different options in light of what you now know about the whole design.

- Prioritize according to what users want most, but implement according to what is most realistic for you. You will not be able to do everything that users want, so understand how you can give them a design that meets as many of their requirements as possible within a workable implementation framework.

- Look beyond the next stage to see if some actions might make more sense in later iterations. If you cannot accomplish everything in the next phase, think about which changes might be postponed. Analyze which changes make sense to develop and test together and which might be better addressed either alone or in combination with other later features.

- Think about what you might learn from users in the next phase. It might be that you need to structure the design to get feedback on something rather than directly solve a problem. If there isn't a way to solve every problem, think about how to best gather additional information that will support your problem-solving process.

Exercise task

Using the results of your user tests and the design recommendations you generated in Chapter 7, decide what you will do next. Think about all of your recommendations together and understand the implications for your implementation. Some important considerations:

- Which are the most important items to address? Which might be postponed?

- Are there any recommendations that preclude others? If so, which are more important, and can you see an alternative for those you cannot address as given?

- Are you working within time or other constraints? Understand your constraints so you can plan accordingly. Even if your schedule is not constrained, estimate a time limit for your project to help you understand what you are trying to accomplish.

- Who do you have available on the design team to help carry out whatever plan you put into place? Your available resources might dictate what you can or can't do.

- If there is anything you are choosing not to address now, how will you keep a record of your decision so that you can refer to it later?

Method 2: Scheduling the Iteration

To allocate time and resources to your "next-step plan" to ensure that it will be carried through.

While you probably thought about the time frame of your next iteration when your were deciding what to do, there is a real benefit to drafting a more concrete schedule for development. As discussed in the Planning and Scheduling section in Chapter 6 on prototyping, the primary benefits of a time-table are directed progress and a design that specifically addresses necessary issues and problems. Scheduling an iteration, however, is more focused in that you address a single stage in your design, with known goals and action items that can be generated from those goals and your available resources. Be as specific as possible when scheduling the iteration because you have a real plan to incorporate and real tasks to accomplish.

Examine the relationship among tasks

Consider the relationship among your action tasks. Think about which will have to precede others, and which might take place simultaneously. Examine each task in relation to the others, and think about the next iteration as a whole. Draw a bar graph or other visual representation of the relationship of the tasks if this helps to understand the timing of one activity in terms of all others.

Consider the end product of this iteration

To assess the time associated with the various action items, it might help to consider what you will have when you are done. Certainly you will want to know whether there will be a prototype at the end of this process, and whether you will test it. You should consider the form of the prototype, and whether it will be off- or on-line. Decide on the prototype form most suitable for the design goals you must address, not based on what number iteration you are on or whether you have already done that kind of prototype before.

Think about the goal for your prototype—will you run a user test with it, or evaluate the prototype in a group design session? What you do with the prototype will nearly always have some affect on the time you must spend developing it. Allocate the time to do whatever you think is appropriate—don't just start at some arbitrary time and work until time runs out. Having a schedule will let you best manage and accomplish each step.

Plan around resources

Understand from the start how much time and what resources are necessary to carry out each step of your plan. If you have not already done so, assign an approximate total time to each task in your action-item list. If a task is particularly long, identify milestones to break it up into achievable chunks.

Besides estimating each step in your action-item list, think about team-member responsibilities and other resources that you must allocate. Assign responsibilities for each task. Write down the names of the people who will be responsible for each task. Note the resources or materials that might be necessary for each job.

If team members hold conflicting expectations of task delivery, change your action list or schedule. Even if all tasks can be spaced adequately, you might be relying too heavily on some member of the design team who cannot possibly accomplish all that you have doled out. Or perhaps the plan is unrealistic in that it requires running tasks on the same piece of computer hardware that cannot reasonably support such simultaneous development. These are the kinds of issues you want to address in determining the overall schedule for your design iteration.

The importance of scheduling the iteration

As with deciding what to do, scheduling your iteration takes a little time. However, the time devoted to scheduling is valuable in helping you through this phase of development and thus your overall product. Scheduling the iteration is important because it can:

Make the most of the time and resources available.

Until you put down on paper how you really plan to spend your time and make use of personnel and other resources, you will rarely be able to understand all the interrelations and your overall expectations. Because assessing all of these needs in a schedule will help address how resources will be used, it will let you make the most of the time and resources available. You might discover conditions you were previously unaware of. If problems are caught early enough in this development cycle, you can adequately address them and save yourself later trouble.

Help you foresee impossible goals and revise accordingly.

Even when we think we have considered every possible detail of the design, we often find as we get into the process that we have overlooked something critical that keeps us from accomplishing our goals. Writing down each task, the people responsible for it, and other resources will help ensure that you really are addressing the critical details. Making assumptions about your design without understanding all of the factors can result in a costly mistake. You don't want to compromise the quality of your user interface. You'll avoid this by mapping out as much as possible at the start.

Understand team member roles.

Think about which team member will be responsible for which tasks. This not only helps you make sure that everything gets done, it also ensures that everyone on the design team is involved to his or her maximum potential. If you do not spell out who will do what, team members might make erroneous assumptions about what they should be doing and what others will do. This might lead to duplicate effort, or worse, the oversight of some critical actions. Let all team members express what they believe they are best suited to do, and make assignments according to skills, preferences, and overall schedule considerations.

Set the basis for the next stage of iteration.

Knowing what you will do in the next stage and having a plan for accomplishing it is almost as good as having it all done. A schedule will provide a strong foundation for carrying out your design. When questions arise or conflicts occur, you can refer to the schedule and understand how the resolution you choose might affect the overall design. Without such a schedule, meeting your final goals given the changes you choose to make will be a gamble. Having a schedule won't guarantee your work gets done on time, but it will establish a continuing basis for evaluation and provide a way to keep the development process on track.

Steps for scheduling the iteration

1. Next to each of the items in your action list, estimate the time needed to carry it out. Write the name of the person who will be responsible for the task and the resources to be used.

2. If necessary, chart or graph the relationships of the action items to time and people responsible to get a better overall picture. Understand the progression of the design that must take place, and any interdependencies.

3. Look at all your deliverables, dates, and people responsible. Put an overall time frame on this phase of development.

4. Check your schedule against any constraining factors. See that your schedule is realistic, and not too time-consuming.

5. If the schedule indicates any overlap or impossibilities, correct it. If you are constrained by time, cut out additional action items. If you have additional time, go back to your list of secondary action items and consider including them. Or allot more time to the items you have listed.

6. Produce a final schedule listing each action item, when it will be completed, and who will be responsible. Use this schedule as a reference during development. While it might change, it will be useful in understanding development ramifications.

Hints/suggestions

*   Use comparisons with previous experience to help you gauge time. Talk with others who have had similar experiences.

- When you have no point of reference, try to gather as much information as possible: what are the design implications and steps, how many people will be involved, and do you have everything you need to carry out an action item? An estimate of total time will help determine overall scheduling.

- Use graphical approaches to understand interrelationships—either on-line applications or simple sketches can help identify key relationships in your design that words alone might not be able to.

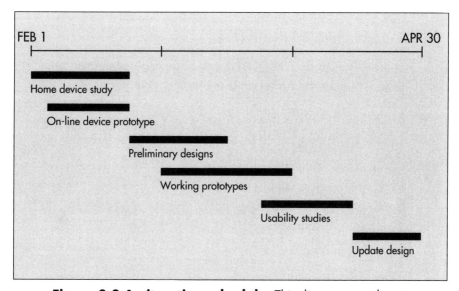

Figure 8.2 An iteration schedule. This diagram graphs out the various stages of an early iteration for a design. Note that user studies and on-line explorations are planned to occur simultaneously. When they are complete, design can begin. Implementation starts sometime after design begins, and the last month is dedicated to user testing and updating the design. User testing actually begins some time before the prototype has been fully implemented, to allow for test planning.

Exercise task

Take your list of action items describing what you will do and map them out in an appropriate schedule. In your schedule, present the order in which the tasks will be completed (including which might be completed in parallel), time frames and dates for each task, who will be responsible for carrying them out, and any necessary resources that must be allocated to accomplish the task (particularly computer hardware or other equipment). Think about the following:

- What is your overall time frame? You probably can project one, even if you don't have specific time or delivery constraints.

- What is the relative importance of each task to the others? Allocate more time and resources to more important tasks.

- What is the relative difficulty of the tasks to each other? Realize that more difficult tasks will require more time.

- Are there potential conflicts that require you to rethink certain tasks? You might not be able to accomplish all that you had hoped because of time or resource constraints. If so, use your best judgment to include those tasks you believe to be more important.

- Will a graphic approach help you to understand the relationship among tasks, and which might be accomplished simultaneously? If so, draw a chart or graph.

Method 3: Testing Again

To conduct additional usability tests that allow you to check changes made to alleviate problems from a previous test, or to incorporate additional elements of your design.

In most cases, you will tailor your iteration so that you create some kind of prototype that can be presented to users for feedback. Many iteration phases end in a user testing procedure, where you present the results of your revised design. In fact, since you have probably made changes based on feedback from earlier user sessions, additional user tests are even more valuable than the originals for seeing if the changes made are appropriate. Testing again confirms the design changes and helps you see if you are progressing toward a more usable design.

Successive testing is in fact integral to the iterative process of design. The primary reason you iterate in user interface software design is to continually improve your system or application according to what users want or expect. You find out what users want in your user testing sessions. So your iteration is about creating a design, showing it to users, incorporating any feedback they give in a new design, testing again, and so on. The process can continue for quite some time. You obviously cannot iterate infinitely for each system you develop. Often two-to-four iterations will reveal the system's most critical flaws.

Choosing test participants

Your additional user tests might involve the same users who participated in earlier tests, or perhaps completely different participants. The people you involve in your tests will depend on many factors. In most cases, it is best to bring in new participants for the tests. Even if you are building a specialized system, or one that relies on repeat users, you will probably benefit more in the early developmental stages of your design from having fresh points of view presented by new participants.

It might be, of course, that you bring back participants for a repeat testing session because they are appropriate, or because you must, due to limited access to additional participants. Who you can engage as users, particularly for repeat tests, will depend on who is available to you, the nature of your system or application, the types of users you are seeking, and what you want to learn from your tests. In the last round of testing, for instance, it might be appropriate to bring back previous users who can help you address the user interface issues significant to repeat users.

Choosing test tasks

The tasks you give your users in testing might be the same as those in earlier tests or they might be new ones. This too will depend on a number of factors, including your goals for this test (and whether they are the same or revised from a previous test), the specific features and functions you are addressing, what you hope to learn, who your users are, and the nature of your system.

If you are testing a new approach to a problem that surfaced in a previous design stage, you should probably use the same task to check your revised design. If you change the task, you risk not adequately answering the question. However, if you are exploring an alternative approach to a design based on user feedback, then it might be appropriate to come up with an alternative task.

Reuse test components when possible

It is evident that retesting your design is not always as simple as running the same test over again. However, you can often benefit greatly from using the components of a previous test that make the most sense for your revised design. The best way to evaluate how much of the test to reuse is to think about the goals of your design. What did you hope to accomplish in the earlier iteration, and how many of those goals hold for the revised design as well? You might need only minimal revision in your test to alter it to the point where it is useful for the next design.

Using focus groups to evaluate redesigns

Another strategy to retesting is to bring back users from previous tests specifically to evaluate whether design changes address the concerns they expressed in the earlier tests. Such an evaluative procedure really isn't a user test, because the users know too much about the system and because you aren't really giving them tasks to test the redesign.

Consider bringing together a number of previous participants as a focus group. Present the new design to them as a group and ask specifically for feedback on redesigned features. Focus groups are not the ideal way to conduct your user testing of new designs, since they don't provide users with a realistic experience for interaction and don't allow them to use the system as they really might. Also, putting numerous people together can affect the type of feedback you get as compared to feedback from one-on-one situations. However, for certain redesign evaluations, the group dynamics created by a focus group might actually yield more information as people build on the ideas of others. Whether to use focus groups for evaluation of a design revision depends on your design, time constraints, and resources.

The importance of testing again

Testing again is critical to iterative software design for many reasons. Use retesting so that you can:

Check your design decisions.

As noted, testing again is the most reliable way of checking that design changes improve the system. If users are not brought in to offer feedback on the changes, there is no guarantee that the decisions you made were appropriate. You might have in fact worsened the design rather than improved it. Ideally, bringing in users to retest the design can confirm that your changes are successful, although this scenario is not always the case. More likely, additional tests will help you evaluate whether you are headed in the right direction and whether you have reduced the severity of the problems identified.

```
                    Home Library System
                    Usability Test 1

                         TASKS

    1. Identify what you think this system may be used
       for.  What do each of the elements you see on the
       screen mean to you?  What does the overall screen
       make you think of?

    2. How would you search for an item in the library?
       What types of references are available to you?
       Look for a book written by the author
       James Joyce.

    3. Once you have found a book by Joyce, would this
       system allow you to store a local copy of it?
       Explain how you might like this system to support
       this feature.

    4. Does this system support searching for more than
       one item at a time?  Say, for example, you want
       to find all books written by living American
       presidents.  How would you use this system
       to do this?

    5. Find out what individual tools may be available
       to you.
```

Figure 8.3 Successive user tests showing progression of the design. These two user tests for the same system show the progression of the Home Library design. The first test aims to explore general system issues, such as basic search techniques and organization of screen elements, and presents tasks to prompt

```
                    Home Library System
                    Usability Test 2

                         TASKS

    1. Look for a book written by author James Joyce.

    2. Store a local copy of this book so that next time
       you want it you do not have to go through the
       same search procedure.

    3. Find all books written by living American
       presidents.  Since this is the kind of request
       you have often, see if there is a way to store
       this request so you do not have to make it again
       next time you want it.

    4. Flip through the Joyce book you located before.
       Leave a bookmark at the start of chapter 3.

    5. The librarian has left you a list of references
       you requested last week.  Find this list.
```

the user to do so. The second test presents tasks which revisit the search techniques to check on the design update in the next iteration, but in a more focused way since general impressions aren't as important. It also introduces some additional features which were too focused for the first version of the test.

See if you have further or different problems.

As you change the features and retest them, you might find that you better define the problems users have, or that there are further—or even different—problems than you originally identified. At the same time as you evaluate the progress made on problems identified in earlier tests, you will use successive revisions to introduce additional issues to your design. New features and refinements can also be addressed in successive tests, to help you identify if there are additional concerns.

Confirm your choices.

When you have questions about which design approach might best address problems identified in earlier user tests, successive tests can help you confirm design decisions. You can choose to incorporate one alternative in the design itself; if users react favorably to it, then you probably have found a solution. However, you run the risk that the implemented alternative is not appropriate and then you have missed the opportunity for feedback on other possibilities.

You can present more than one alternative to users in the tests, either by incorporating one and discussing the other, or by mocking up more than one choice and obtaining user feedback. Try to present the alternatives as actual tasks to allow users to interact with your approaches. Having various choices available might help them identify the best one.

Contribute to a more robust design.

Successive iterations of user tests will lead you to a more robust and successful design. Even if you experience some frustration at negative feedback from users in a certain iteration, successive iterations will help guide you to a design that best meets user needs. In the long run, you will have designed a well-tuned system aimed at doing what users want it to do in a way that makes sense to them.

Steps for testing again

1. Prepare your prototype for user testing. Incorporate changes identified in your action list from previous iterations.

2. Generate goals for this user test. Consider what you want to know, independent of any tests before.

3. Review goals from previous tests. Check them against your current goals to see that your progressive goals make sense. Revise your current goals if necessary.

4. Generate tasks that will address your current goals. You might be able to recycle tasks from a previous test.

5. Consider who you will use as test participants. Is it appropriate to include the same users from last time? Should you recruit users who have no prior experience with your application? Some of both? You might want to hold focus groups rather than individual user tests to get general feedback from previous users, then conduct individual tests with new users.

Hints/suggestions

Take advantage of work you have already done—there's nothing heroic about creating brand new tasks for every test unless it is appropriate.

Take the time to evaluate whether repeat or fresh participants would be better. If you are testing a change that you made in response to user requests, you might want to ask the users who requested the change what they think. On the other hand, you might be testing a new approach and want a fresh and "untainted" pool of users to provide input. Also keep in mind that although retesting the same users might be necessary, the tasks you present might be affected: using the same participants with the same tasks often will not provide motivation to users to tell you what you need to know.

Remember to check that problems from your earlier tests have been resolved with your design changes. Successive tests should reveal less critical problems. For example, if earlier tests show general confusion with navigation of the overall interface, later tests might show users don't recognize individual icons for linking locations. The nature of the problems should improve; if you still have the same broad problems, your design solutions are not working and you need to identify and incorporate users' responses to these problems.

Exercise task

Plan and, if possible, conduct user tests for your next iteration. (You might have to actually put to use your plan from the previous exercise and implement that iteration before you can conduct the tests!) Make use of many of the general user testing methodologies presented in Chapter 7. Some of your considerations in planning these tests should include:

- What are the goals of this test? Which functions or interactive methods are you trying to test?

- What tasks will direct users to address your goals? Will they be similar to tasks you might have used in earlier tests, or new ones?

- Who and how many users will you test this time? Where will you find these users?

- Have you changed your test significantly from earlier tests? Why or why not?

- Is your testing process evolving so that you are actually refining your design in successive iterations? It should be; if not, evaluate your testing approach to make sure you are obtaining and heeding user advice.

Method 4: Knowing When to Stop

To understand when your design has evolved to the point that further iterative design cycles will not be worth the effort, so that you are effectively done.

Many iterative design cycles end because of time limits imposed by scheduling constraints or delivery dates. However, not all design iteration approaches are constrained by such factors, and even those that are can be better controlled if you can estimate the ideal time to stop iterations. Even in open-ended research projects, you cannot iterate forever, nor do you want to. It is not always easy to identify the right time to stop, but some considerations can help make the process easier. Basically, you want to continue until the problems subside, the nature of the problems shifts significantly, or as long as time allows.

Use the allotted time well

The trick in iterating is not to stop because you have run out of time, but to use wisely the time you have—to make enough progress in your design within the allotted time. There will probably always be another iteration you could do that would improve your design; but when the iterations end, the hope is that the existing design is so stable and robust that any further changes would make only marginal difference.

Signs to watch for

When one or both of these situations develops, you can be confident that you are reaching the end of iterative cycling:

User testing reveals minimal problems.

When problems are minor and don't concern users much, this is a sign that your design has evolved fairly well. This is particularly true when you compare these problems to those identified in your first iteration and find that there is a significant difference in the degree of importance. If you have solved the general problems introduced early on (such as a misunderstanding of a navigational model) and now see small discrepancies (such as wishing a particular function was called something else), your design has come a long way, and you are nearing the end.

Users give overwhelmingly positive feedback.

This is especially noticeable if such feedback was lacking in early designs and user tests. For the most part, user test participants seem to be a critical lot—they tell you what is wrong with the system much more often than what is right. (Be careful to assume this of every user, though, since some people don't have it in their nature to criticize, and will hold back from telling you anything negative. Weigh user feedback as a whole for your tests, and chances are that the positive participants will be outnumbered by those telling you what's wrong with your system.) If most users are giving you fairly optimistic feedback about the system, it's a good sign.

When the time or money runs out

Of course, you won't always be able to work on the design up to the time when significant problems give way to small inconveniences or when the users love your system. There are times when you have to stop because time or money has run out. If you have applied a user-centered design process to your work, you will know that you have at least made the most of your development time.

Try to plan ahead and get in enough iterations to make this evolution in the time that you have—even if it means iteration stages significantly shorter than what you had hoped. Then when you must stop designing, you can feel good that you built a user-centered system despite the time constraints.

Evaluating your progress

Before you actually cease the iterations, it is important to evaluate whether your design is successful enough to put it to use in an actual system. It is a sad fact of software development that we cannot always deliver the product we hope to. Use the user-oriented criteria discussed throughout this book to assess if you have created a successful system that responds to users' needs.

If your most recent tests show serious problems or misunderstanding with the user interface, you might want to re-evaluate whether this product is ready to go simply because your time is up. You can even use the state of the user interface as an argument to present to the right people to sway them to give you additional time or resources. In the worst case—that is, if your latest testing results are so negative that you risk alienating users or making a bad name for yourself—you might have to opt for not seeing the project through. Knowing how to evaluate the progress of your design can help in your business practices as well.

The importance of knowing when to stop

Knowing when to stop iterating is important because it can:

Save you from needless additional work.

While it is true that you can always continue with another design iteration, the bottom line is that you might not have to. Even if your design is not constrained by project milestones or product delivery dates, you probably don't want to do any work you don't have to. Rarely is there only one way to present software functionality or interaction, and thus successive iterations might help you continue to generate alternatives. But these alternatives might prove to be of equal value after a certain point. Knowing how to evaluate when you can stop iterating can help you avoid cycling needlessly through additional alternatives.

Help you evaluate your progress.

It is possible to get into an iteration rut, where you continue to iterate your design just because you have been doing it for so long. Taking the time to evaluate whether you should continue, instead of simply plodding ahead, can help you to assess where you are and the significance of the progress you have made. Knowing the criteria that should determine if you should go on can help you evaluate this progress.

Turn research into product.

Software designs built using iterative design methodologies are often regarded as research works, particularly when they are not bound by product delivery dates. However, if you are conducting software design research, knowing when your design has evolved sufficiently might aid you in turning that research into product. If you have made significant progress and your design solves the problems it set out to, it's time to consider the next step of product development. Knowing the criteria by which to evaluate if your design has arrived is critical to accomplishing this.

Illustrate the success of your iterative process.

When you know that it is time to stop iterating, you are not simply recognizing that you have done enough design work. You are seeing that the iterative process you put into place has helped you achieve successful design. Designs that meet user needs, that are not threatening, that do not pose major problems, and, most important, that can be used by real people to accomplish real tasks are testimony to a process based on structuring the design around the user.

Steps for knowing when to stop

1. Work within the bounds of any scheduling constraints you have. Be aware of when you might have to stop.

2. Evaluate the problems revealed in your latest user tests. If you have earlier tests to compare these results with, do so.

3. You might not have fewer problems, but they should be less critical. They will, for instance, illustrate user complaints about specific detailed functions or features rather than general structure or functionality.

4. Assess if an additional iteration and testing would be worth your while. How sure are you of any changes you might make? How much do you stand to gain?

5. Determine the effects of not making any further changes to your design. If there isn't a serious downside to not making changes, it might not be worth your while to make them.

Hints/suggestions

- Listen to what your users say about the system or application. If their complaints or problems are overwhelmed by their positive reactions to and favorable statements about the software, then the problems probably are those users could live with. On the other hand, if problems seem small but users state they aren't really crazy about the software, there are probably additional broader problems that you are missing (and unfortunately this indicates that you are not yet done).

- Try not to let time determine when you will stop iterating. From the beginning, plan for multiple iterations in the time you have, even if it means shortened stages. This way, you will complete iterations when you are ready, not simply when time runs out.

- Solicit input from other team members. They can help you determine whether the test results indicate that there is no need to test again, or what the ramifications of another iterative cycle will be. You might all decide there is time for another iteration, or convince each other that another cycle is not necessary.

Exercise task

Evaluate your current design based on the results of your latest user test and determine if the design is complete. (You might want to go through another iteration of the design and then do this exercise. If you do additional iterations, assess the design to see if you should stop at the end of each cycle, as it will help you understand the overall progress of your design.) Criteria that should be considered include:

- What are the problems most recently identified? How do they compare with earlier problems? Is the nature of the problems similar, or less critical?

- What is the feedback you are getting from users? Are test participants telling you they love the system and want it tomorrow (even if it does have some problems), or are they saying they don't really see themselves using it?

- How much time do you reasonably have ahead of you for development, and what can you hope to accomplish in that time?

- Is additional development worth your while at this time? What do you stand to gain from another iteration? What do you stand to lose?

Chapter 9

Applying the User-Oriented Design Process

User interface design is the kind of process that develops over a long period. It is highly likely that the you have been exposed to—and perhaps have experience with—many of the concepts presented in this book. Even if you don't think of yourself as a user interface designer, you probably have had some experience designing a user interface—if not in software design, then for some other product used by people. My hope is that this book will encourage you to incorporate these techniques more thoroughly in the software design you already do, and maybe think about software design in a new light.

Whether you already have a familiar software design process or are developing entirely new skills, you will probably follow a similar approach to applying the techniques introduced in the previous chapters. In a general sense, you should combine the techniques that work best for you and your particular software. At first it might not be obvious which of the techniques are appropriate, and you might invest some time up front learning how to make the different methodologies work within your framework.

You will not always apply the same combination of techniques for each project, but you will find that you have favorites that seem to work best for you. User-centered design methodologies are presented in a range of types so that they can be flexible and adapted to a process you can use in your work. At the very least, apply them to do what you can to make your software more usable and approachable.

Demonstrating Process Viability to Others

In nearly all cases, your goal will be to develop your software to the point where it supports appropriate functionality in a way that users can understand and apply. Particularly in your early attempts to apply user-oriented design, you will probably have another goal as well: to make the people you work with and work for more aware of the importance and feasibility of this process.

You will probably work just as hard at establishing the viability of the process as you will at developing the software itself. While having to prove the viability of the techniques might be distracting and add time to your overall development process, it shouldn't take that much more time than simply using the processes to develop your software.

You will see the value of applying the techniques through the improvements in your software and the benefits of incorporating user feedback. Document the process so that you can demonstrate this value to others. In a short time, they will see that incorporating user-oriented methodologies is well worth any added effort early on, and that the benefits will simply increase as you become more adept with this approach.

Integration with Traditional Software Design

Many software developers are taught a traditional software life cycle, or a basic procedure for software design and development. This typical software development approach follows a procedure something like that shown in Figure 9-1.

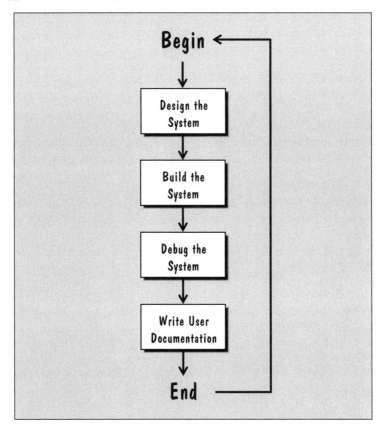

Figure 9-1 Traditional software development process.
This simple flow chart illustrates the software life cycle process as conventionally taught in many software development programs. Note that the user is not mentioned in the process until the very end, and that the actions of the process focus on the software itself.

Unfortunately, such a process takes the user into account only at the end of the cycle. The approach of the traditional software life cycle seems to be: develop a system and then tell the user how to use it. We can adapt this software development process so the methodologies presented in Chapters 3 through 8 are incorporated within this framework. It means changing the approach to software design somewhat, but if we look at this new approach within the existing structure, then maybe the benefits will be evident and change will not seem as threatening. The approaches to including the user-oriented techniques in such a software development process are discussed below.

Critical steps for system design

The traditional software development process focuses primarily on the software itself; the design effort focuses more on how the system does what it does rather than what it does and the specifics of the interaction and user interface. Clearly, the implementation of the system is important, and is not meant to be slighted by focusing on the user interface. However, the implementation should follow from the appropriate functionality and interaction of the system.

The "Design the System" step in Figure 9-1 should probably be the longest in the overall process, encompassing early user studies, off- and on-line prototypes, usability testing if appropriate, and finally actual software implementation design. This is because, typically, you will want to conduct these early efforts of user-oriented design before you begin implementation. In the case of the blended traditional/user-oriented process, it is before the traditional software development cycle really begins. Design the software appropriate for users, and the design of the implementation will follow.

Include the techniques wherever possible

The design stage is not the only one where user-oriented techniques might be applied. Even if you cannot incorporate these methodologies in the software design—either because you come into the project too late or there is too much resistance from others involved—you can still introduce them in other stages. When you are building the system, for instance, you can conduct usability tests and present findings from user feedback to help resolve questions about the implementation or make other developmental decisions. You might also be able to present usability tests as part of the debugging process, if you think of debugging the user interface as part of the overall debugging procedure.

Usability testing methodologies are not the only ones appropriate in these stages, but often are the most readily accepted or adapted. Once you have shown the value of incorporating findings from usability tests, you can present other techniques, such as broader user studies or prototyping methods, to help solve some of the problems you might have uncovered.

Use the techniques to increase awareness

The hardest part of incorporating the user-oriented methodologies into a traditional software development process probably will be changing the politics of the system. You have to obtain agreement from others that the user-centered techniques are appropriate, and get support for adapting the current approach to include the new tools. Use the techniques wherever you can; when you do, draw attention to your successes to increase overall awareness of their appropriateness and capabilities.

One way to do this is through documentation of the processes used. This is especially appropriate for findings from user studies or tests, or to record the evolution of a design over time. However, documents might not be convincing enough by themselves—they do not get read or their message is not communicated with enough power. Using videotapes of user sessions to directly point out user problems might be more effective. Videotapes of people trying to use software but having serious problems can convince even the most skeptical software developers that changes are necessary.

If videotaping is not possible, audio tapes might provide similar benefits. Even still photographs or illustrated storyboards documenting the problems can help augment a written description. Present the work that you have done, in person if possible, to communicate your message directly. Do whatever you can to let others see the benefit in spending the necessary time and effort in a user-oriented approach to design. Even if you do not make significant changes in your current system, over time your message will begin to be heard, and you will gain support for changing the process.

Test software within its known constraints

Usability testing is the most obvious way to "break in" to the traditional software development process. You can probably conduct usability tests with the software, whatever its condition or progress toward completion. Even if there are obvious flaws in the system that cannot be changed, you can improve the existing system by obtaining user feedback and reacting to it. This might prove somewhat frustrating, especially if the flaws might have been avoided with better design methodologies. But remember that you can develop a much improved, more usable interface by bringing in users no matter the stage.

Conducting a usability test just once, even if it is too late to make significant changes, can make the development team aware of its value. On the next project, you are almost sure to gain support for your usability tests, and probably much earlier in the development process than you were able to accomplish this first time.

When Another Process is Already in Place

The traditional software development process illustrated in Figure 9-1 is clearly not the only system people use. Adapting the techniques presented in the earlier chapters to any existing process can be beneficial. Many of the previous suggestions still apply. In addition, the following tips will help you deal with general adaptation of the methodologies.

Work within the constraints of that process

The more you challenge the existing procedures, the more resistance you will probably encounter. Work within the constraints of the particular process you are trying to influence. Examine the process and understand where time allows for the appropriate procedures, as well as where they can do the most good. Talk to the development team to understand what constraints they might be working under, and which constraints might decide how to best apply user-centered methodologies.

Assess all stages

Take a good look at the process under way. Review any existing documentation of the process, such as an organization-wide policy. Evaluate the stages that are prescribed, and assess which might be the most appropriate for incorporating some of the user-centered approaches. Knowledge of the process will help you communicate with those who formed the existing policies, and better prepare you for any discussions about how or why user-based design for software development is appropriate.

When you are trying to introduce the techniques to a process already under way, explore particularly the current stage of the design, as well as the remaining stages in the process. This way, you can make an immediate recommendation on how to adapt your techniques, and hope to make a difference no matter what stage you begin in.

Evaluate which techniques are appropriate and feasible

Take the time to think about which of the techniques make the most sense for the existing design, for your organization, and for the process as a whole. Consider what might be missing from the current process that can be provided by the various user-centered techniques. If you don't know enough about what users want before development begins, early user studies are probably appropriate. If you find that much time is wasted on the visual layout of the design or the nature of the interactive elements, more time invested in off-line designs that address these design considerations would be valuable.

Also consider which techniques are most feasible in your organization—
where do you have skills to provide the methodologies and what other
resources might be available to you? While practically any user-centered
design approach will help your process, there are probably some that would
make more of an impact. Introducing these first will not only improve your
process, but also your credibility as a user-centered designer when your recommendations prove valuable.

Be willing to do the work yourself

Pointing out better methods and helping others in your organization to understand how to apply those methods can improve your approach to software
design. However, simply being a mouthpiece for these ideas might not be
enough when your audience understands the value but isn't able or willing
to provide the necessary resources. One of the best ways to support your own
ideas is to be ready to take action.

Volunteer to be the one to conduct the necessary work. Give up your current
responsibilities for those that will help champion these techniques, or, if you
have to, take on additional responsibilities to get the work done. Even if in the
short term you must work extra hours or in an area that is not directly your
responsibility, you might discover in the long run that you are able to convince
others of the value of your ideas and change the process or team skills.

Dealing with Schedule Limitations

Sometimes it is not the process in place or the people for whom you work
that impede you. You simply might not have adequate time to apply the
process all the way through. Identify the time you do have, so you know what
you are working with. Then taking the following steps might help you to
obtain critical results with a scaled-back version of the techniques.

Analyze where to apply the methodologies

If there isn't the time to undertake the design the way you would like, understand where the techniques can be most effective. Look at the type of design problem you are trying to solve and the nature of your users. Consider where user input will be most important. Come up with an effective subset of the techniques, and prioritize them in your design process. You might not be able to apply them all, but at least you will know which ones you intend to. If more time becomes available, you might be able to include others.

Scale back on testing

All of the techniques take time, but some take much more than others. It is difficult to reduce the time dedicated to off or on-line prototypes—creating and building the designs is often a time-consuming process. Usability testing, however, has many components that might be scaled back. Rather than eliminating usability testing altogether, cut back on the time by reducing the number of user tests or the length of the tests so you can plan for fewer tasks. Some testing is better than none. Bring in only three or four people to evaluate your software when it isn't feasible to include the nine or ten you want.

Keep your design simple

One way to try to accomplish as much of the overall process as possible is to guard against having too many features or details to develop and test. Keeping your design simple will keep each stage of the design short, and allow you to try out and employ as many of the techniques as possible. Simple designs typically require fewer iterations to solve problems and present all features to users, so you will keep your total time shorter.

Developing a purposefully simple design might not be ideal for your specific system, particularly if early research shows that users want complexity and depth from it. However, it is better to have a simple system in which all components have been adequately explored and in which users can understand the interface than to have a complex system that is partially developed and not adequately tested.

Limiting the feature set or the complexity of the interaction might not be appropriate in an ideal development scenario, but when time is limited it might direct the usability of your product. If you won't be able to have an elaborate process where feedback can come more often from more iterations, then keep it simple.

When You Don't Have Support from Your Organization

Often the biggest obstacle to putting this process into action is not the difficulty of understanding and applying new techniques, or limits in time or budget, but your organization or management. Here are some suggestions for putting the process to work when you don't have official support.

Do it anyway

If you cannot apply the process in the way that you would like to, consider other more roundabout ways. One might be to solicit support from others on your team, and see if together you can find a way to incorporate at least a few of the methodologies into your current process. Even if you don't have the support of your organization or manager, having colleagues who back up your decisions will prove encouraging and helpful.

Another approach is to do what you can in any spare time you have, even after hours if necessary. It might seem like a sacrifice when you aren't being compensated for your work, but chances are that once the work is done, you can use it to get the support you need for other applications of these techniques. The risk is that your work will not be appreciated and that you might waste your time, but more likely than not you will be building a better product as a result of your efforts. Even if your attempts to apply the process are not rewarded by others, the better design you produce will be reward itself.

Demonstrate feasibility

Don't underestimate the power of educating others—showing people what you have done and why it works can help you gain support for your effort. Use documentation of findings and associated changes made in your user interface, audio tapes or videotapes of user testing segments (particularly as they relate to specific problems with an existing or prior system), and demonstrations of your prototypes to show others how your design process has benefited your work.

It might take some extra time to gather the materials, but you will already have done most of the hard part—generating the content—during your user interface development process. The effort you spend putting that material in a form that others can readily comprehend might pay off in winning over the support you need to include more of these techniques in future designs.

Expect to make small advances with time

Change takes time, particularly when it involves well-established development procedures. When you encounter resistance from your organization or management, you must expect that it will take time to achieve any success in persuading them to incorporate these novel approaches in their software design. Continue to talk about and demonstrate the advantages of the various methods. Practice those that you can, and always look for ways to introduce them into your routine. Be persistent, and slowly but surely you will realize your goals.

Choose to Do What Works for You

Even if you encounter no resistance, have all the time in the world, and there is no existing process in place, it might not make sense to try to apply all the methodologies for every one of your designs. Sometimes success means applying only some of them. Choose the parts of the process that make the most sense for you. Suggestions on how to do this follow.

Analyze the current process

As discussed previously, look carefully at what you now do to develop user interfaces for your software. Think about which of the user-oriented techniques are needed in your development process and which would be the most valuable. Do you need to spend more time in early design stages, or devote more effort to building small on-line prototypes that showcase potential interaction techniques? Consider the kinds of problems that typically show up in the systems you develop. Where might it make the most sense to bring in users to give you input on your designs? Familiarize yourself with the various techniques, and with your own product and process in mind, determine those that make the most sense for you.

Start where you are comfortable

Starting with a few of the techniques rather than all of them at once will help you adapt them into your work style. Some methods are probably more familiar to you, or make use of skills you believe you can provide with minimal effort. You might want to include these in your user interface development process first. If you have some drawing skills, some of the off-line techniques such as storyboarding might come easily to you. If you are a trained programmer, try adapting some on-line prototyping methods the first time you attempt a user-centered design approach.

Not only will techniques that make use of your skills be easier for you to adapt, they will help you to feel more comfortable with the overall process because you will build confidence in your abilities quickly. You can eventually include a wider range of methods, and expand on your process. Soon you will feel comfortable with even the procedures that do not rely on skills in which you were trained. You will be able to extend your process to include any techniques that make sense for your designs.

Continue to introduce methods

If you start with only a subset of the methodologies, be persistent about using others as they become applicable or as time allows. You will begin to feel comfortable with those techniques over time, but do not fall into the rut of using them exclusively. Introducing new techniques will help you gain familiarity and comfort with them as well. For example, introduce just one new method in each design you undertake, or one every couple of designs. You will expand your repertoire of capabilities and grow as a user interface software developer.

It might be worthwhile at first to introduce new methods even when you don't see a direct need for that approach, just to get some experience with it. Clearly, you will not be able to introduce new techniques in each design you develop unless time and resources allow it. However, practice with a new method will improve on your design, and prepare you for a time in which your experience with this method will be needed.

Don't try to do too much

It is a rare individual who will be able to apply all of the methods presented here in a single design and succeed at every one. Especially if you have never used any of these approaches before, it will be extremely difficult to make them all work together in a smooth and useful way. (The application of all the methods to the supermarket guide exercise in this book is a learning process and is not intended to advocate the suitability of using all methods for a single design.) Trying to accomplish too much, particularly in your first experiences with these techniques, might only frustrate you and keep you from succeeding in any of them. Start small—you will learn the methods more thoroughly and design better software as a result.

Chapter 10

Extending the User-Oriented Design Process

The techniques presented in Chapters 3 through 8 are not a closed, linear process for user interface software development. Rather, they are a set of methodologies that, when applied in the right combinations and under the right circumstances, can help produce software that involves the user in its design and thus meets user needs. Different projects will require different combinations of the techniques, and in varying intensities. Some projects might make use of most of them, while others are best served by only one or two. You will understand which combinations make sense for your particular projects as you get more experience with these techniques. The techniques are a foundation for sound user-oriented software development.

The overall process, however, is dynamic—the individual techniques and the process itself can change or be extended when appropriate. You might add techniques to the collection when you discover ones that make sense for user interface design. Of course, you won't automatically incorporate any method you come across. First evaluate the benefits of the new technique. Can you accomplish the same results with techniques you already use?

Be on the look out for methods used in other disciplines that you might adapt to your work. For example, you might find techniques in some of the interdisciplinary fields listed in Chapter 1. In general, look for ways to obtain information from potential users, apply that information to your design, get user feedback on the current design, and incorporated the feedback into your software. The more experience you have with the process, the better you will extend the process in related and goal-oriented ways.

You will not always need to extend the process. Particularly when you first start to practice these methods, you should focus on the ones presented here to help you understand this approach to design. As you gain experience, however, you will know when to build additional practices into the approach.

Extending this process or the techniques might be accomplished in varying ways. It can involve coming up with completely new methods, or building on the methods in this book in ways that make sense for your project. It might happen by bringing in experts or ideas from other discipline areas, or even representatives of your user population to help mold your designs. Some of the choices open to you are explored in the following sections.

Incorporating Other Techniques

One way to extend the overall process is to introduce new methods. Because the user-oriented design process is somewhat informal, it is not at all a contained one. New methodologies might be appropriate, especially for projects involving new technologies or areas where user interface software has not yet been introduced. The following tips can help you recognize the need for new techniques, and how to incorporate them smoothly into your user interface development process.

Evaluate the techniques against each project

Look carefully at each project you undertake to understand what you can gain from applying each of the techniques in Chapters 3 through 8. Consider what each technique offers, and if it can indeed be used for your design. If it isn't right for your project, understand why. Knowing where the approach fails your purpose might help lead you to a new method that provides the desired result. This evaluation will become easier as you get more experience with each technique and can more readily understand how it might or might not apply to a specific project.

Keep in mind the purpose of involving the user

Remember that your aim is to design software that does what users want and need it to do, and in such a way that they can understand how to do it. Methods that enable you to better gather information from your users are certainly appropriate. Be sure to follow the guidelines detailed in Chapters 3 through 8, even if the method you are evaluating is not one included in this book.

Stay objective about the information you interpret from your users and try to remain within the users' natural environment and setting when you conduct studies and tests. Remember that you want to involve users in order to understand their motivations and to help generate creative design ideas. New creative prototyping methods are certainly encouraged, particularly those that help you showcase the concepts of your designs to others. Keep an open mind—any method that supports better design for more usable software might be suitable, even if it doesn't seem to be a conventional software development approach.

Draw on past experience

Your prior experience with other development methods can be extremely valuable, especially those you thoroughly understand and are comfortable executing. If you have practiced some method before, then you will be familiar with what it can or cannot do for you and what you can hope to gain by incorporating it into your software design process.

Consider methods that you used for other purposes, not necessarily only for other software design projects. Think about experiences in social or entertainment situations that might apply to the development of a given software product. For instance, consider a storytelling technique that you might have used with children where you included sound effects as you related the story. It might encourage you to use sound effects in conducting your user tests or your prototyping stages. It might seem far fetched, but any experience you have had communicating with people might actually apply. All your experiences, of course, will not, so evaluate carefully what you can gain from various approaches.

Consider using any method

You might find that methods of any kind—early studies, off- or on-line prototypes, testing or iteration—make sense in a particular design process. You are not limited to expanding only those methods for user research or creative prototyping simply because they might seem the most obvious. The user interface design process is subjective—what works well for one software project might not for another. With time and experience, the decision of whether or not to extend the process for a particular design will become more apparent, as will the appropriate ways to do so. Be true to your users, and you will learn to recognize and incorporate new techniques that work for you and the designs you undertake.

Elaborating on a Single Technique

Rather than add whole new methodologies, it might be enough to build on one of those already in place. You might discover that you want to focus in depth on the one or more techniques that work well for you. You can expand the overall development process by elaborating on a single technique, either adding prescribed steps to those provided or by broadening the scope of its application. Suggestions as to how to expand individual methods are presented next.

User testing as an example

You might have such positive experiences conducting user tests to evaluate your software that you want to expand the procedures and adapt them to a specialized approach of your own. Analyze what you do when you perform user tests, and what does or does not work well for you. If you have a special approach to outlining and defining your test goals, you might want to write those steps directly into the overall test planning process. Be objective about what you do and why it works. Look at your experience over time with more than one project—don't jump to conclusions about changing your approach based on just one experience. If you have consistently applied a new or expanded approach across several designs, your steps are strong candidates for extension into that method.

Follow the needs of your design

You want to extend techniques to make them more useful and possibly more focused, but be careful not to make them too limiting. The techniques presented in Chapters 3 through 8 are kept general so that they can apply across a range of designs. Tailoring them for a particular type of user interface, especially if it is one your work revolves around, can be helpful.

However, recognize that you might not always want to use your customized version. Look at the way you have applied that particular technique across various designs and determine the general steps that you want added to that technique. Keep a record of why you have added these steps, so that at a later time you will have an easier time evaluating if they are appropriate for the specific design you are undertaking.

Learn from others

You can learn from the experiences of others as well as your own experiences. Discuss with colleagues or friends how they design their user interfaces. Even if they do not claim to have been applying a user-oriented approach, there might be something in their development procedure that you can adapt to your own. Seek out others who practice the user-oriented methodologies so that you can learn from their experiences, especially when they have been able to apply techniques that you might not have yet yourself.

Consider forming a user-centered design special interest group in your company or geographic area. Such an organization can be used to share design ideas, and show how and where the process can work for you. Because the user-centered approach is a flexible and growing process, the more examples you have of it working, the better prepared you are to understand it's application.

Research other sources

Be on the lookout not only for other techniques that might be transferred from other sources, but for these user-oriented software techniques under other names or guises. In other disciplinary areas, you might find that similar approaches are used but are referred to differently. Consider disciplines such as advertising, where the user (that is, the consumer) is critical to all of its products. Explore how its user studies are handled, usually through focus groups. Think about its kinds of prototypes, which might be called treatments or presentations.

There are broad similarities in these approaches to those for software design. You can probably learn from the way that these techniques are applied in different fields, particularly if you pay attention both to the similarities and differences. Examining the differences might suggest new ways to apply similar approaches in user interface design.

Revisiting an Older Design

There might be times when you can go back to an old design that was created with a user-centered process and expand on what you did. Perhaps your time on that design was limited and more time has become available, or maybe interest has been sparked for you to renew work on a project that was not well supported then but is now. Whatever the case, you can extend the user interface design process within the scope of the project. It might not involve introducing new or expanded techniques, but rather analyzing what you did then as an overall process and how you might now extend that process based on what you have learned since. Some approaches for extending the existing process follow.

Analyze what worked

Assess the methods you used in your original design. List them, and understand how you benefited from them. What were you able to transfer directly to the next stage of your design? If you worked with others on this design, get their perspectives on the various techniques used. Analyze what each method contributed to the overall process, and how it led to the design that finally evolved.

Analyze why you chose those techniques

Think back to why you picked those techniques. Was it to meet certain design goals, or because of available resources or limited time? Were you simply most familiar with them? Did you choose them because they met the needs of your design, or did you have to compromise because of extenuating circumstances? Were there other techniques you would have rather used in an ideal situation? Are the current conditions—such as time or resources available to you—such that you can now apply alternate methods? Take advantage of your hindsight to see if you can apply other methods, or if you can elaborate on those you already used.

Analyze the results

Look at the results of the individual method applications, such as the findings from user studies or tests, or storyboards, or on-line prototypes. These might help you to remember why you made decisions you did, or if you went on to additional stages with certain preconceptions. Be objective as you analyze what went on at each stage, and assess if you made the right decision for that design or if the decision might have been tempered by some other factor. As you are doing this, try to understand where various other user-oriented techniques would help. Determine where additional work might improve or better direct the design.

Apply subsequent knowledge and experience

Chances are you have completed other designs since you worked on this design. Think about what you have learned and how your process has evolved since then; presumably your designs have progressed across the range of projects. Consider techniques you have been using in more recent designs and whether they might have made sense for this older design. Now that you will be able to continue or extend work on this design, might you borrow any of these techniques? Or are they actually inappropriate for this design based on what you know about them from other designs? Try to learn from all of your projects and experiences with the user-oriented techniques.

Keep track of your process

Keep records of your application of the user interface design process for projects as you undertake them. This will help you during the development of that particular project, since writing down your thoughts or decisions can help clarify them. It will also help if you later revisit that project.

The documentation need not be formal or long—it might even be as simple as brief annotations jotted alongside existing notes or documentation. Consider using a particular pen type or color for all such process recordings, so that you will be able to easily track them later. It might take a little more work on your part during your design, but it will definitely pay off later when you are attempting to review the process you followed and the decisions you made.

When Additional Resources Are Allocated

Often in software development, the allocation of resources changes mid-project. Your resources might become limited and you will have to scale back what you are doing, or you might be fortunate enough to obtain additional resources for your project. This last, happier scenario might be the result when you have been able to demonstrate the benefits of applying the user-oriented design methods early in your process and get the go-ahead from the right parties to expand on your design approach. If more resources are allocated mid-project, there are a number of considerations for expanding your application of the user-oriented design methods.

Examine the original plans

Think about what your original plans for the process were and where you might have had to cut back because of project constraints. If you have documented your plans, this task will of course be easier. Review your reasons for omitting or minimizing the amount of time you were planning to spend on any of the individual techniques. Some of those reasons might no longer hold, especially since more time or resources have now been allocated to this project. Now you will be able to include the techniques or the time you couldn't before (if the reasons why your originally had wanted to include them still hold true).

Analyze the current plan

If you did not compromise in your original plan—or even if you did—analyze what you are currently doing and see what is working well for you thus far. If some of the methods have proven particularly valuable, you might now want to elaborate on them. Spend more time on a particular user study, or draw up storyboards, or expand a flipbook to help you work through aspects of the design that you did not have time for before. Think about ways to incorporate those same types of methods in other stages of this design, or ways that other methods can help build on your findings. With additional time or resources, you might be able to accomplish more than you originally had hoped with the same techniques you were going to use all along.

Analyze current difficulties

Analyze the problems and issues that have arisen over the course of your design. The more time you have spent working on the design, the more concerns you are likely to have. Look for decisions that you made where more information would have been useful. This might justify an additional user study, or spending more time in early design stages building prototypes for design alternatives. Think about the solutions you have devised and whether additional research or design work would be appropriate; note where additional techniques might help. Review the techniques to see if they offer any ideas for expanding on your problem areas. Additional resources or time will almost always help you troubleshoot your design problems.

Use the allocated resources wisely

If more resources are allocated, you should analyze not just where your design process could change from a design perspective, but also the opportunities now available to you. If you are fortunate, the new resources will let you to introduce or build on design methodologies that you could not address before. For instance, if because of an increased budget you now have a graphic designer on your team, you can produce more detailed and complete visual designs.

Even if your new resources do not provide new skills, take advantage of whatever support they do provide. If you have access to additional programmers, perhaps you might be able to build interactive software prototypes for a number of alternative concepts that you could only talk about before. Additional resources might be allocated in the form of equipment; take advantage of it in the way that makes the most sense for your design. Making the best use of who and what are available to you can help you develop high-quality solutions for your designs.

Changing An Existing Framework

When you encounter obstacles from an existing framework for software design, you might be able to put user-oriented techniques into play by expanding on those presented here and including those that mesh more easily with ones in the existing process. Some creative effort might be required on your part to evaluate the methods in place and understand how they might be adapted into the user-centered approaches in a valid and useful way, but doing so might mean getting the support you need for applying these methods. The following information might help you do this.

Start slow if you have to

While you might be anxious to put many of these methods into action, realize that others who are not familiar with them might not share your energy or enthusiasm. You can help win them over by introducing the methods slowly and in small pieces. Casually suggest showing your design to the people who might eventually use it. Point out the places in the existing process where it would be most appropriate to do this, and offer to gather user participants and conduct the sessions. Provide feedback to the design team in supportive ways, even if most of the results were somewhat negative. Next time around, you might be asked to write your user tests directly into the project plan, and you might round up additional support from others for doing so. Even the introduction of just one, or part of one, of the approaches can help make your development more user-centered.

Look for holes in the existing process

Since the techniques presented in this book are approaches to designing software, they probably can be adapted to any design stage of an existing process. You might not want to tell others on your design team your motivation in using these methods, and instead simply introduce elements of them during design sessions. For example, bring paper and pens to a design meeting and draw out or storyboard some of the ideas you hear people discussing. When you hear indecision among meeting participants about how to approach a function or feature, take it as a cue that some research is necessary. Do this research on your own, conducting whatever form of user study makes sense for the particular issue. Bring the results of your findings to the next design meeting. Not only will you provide valuable input for the design, you will impress your colleagues with your creativity and energy!

Plan ahead and start early

While the framework in place might not approach the design problem with a user-oriented slant, chances are you will still have to complete many of the same tasks that you would in a process that practices the user-based techniques. Most software projects involve delivering the software itself along with documentation and other side products. Consider what the end products for your project are, particularly those that end users will see.

If user documentation (such as a user guide) is planned, but it is not in the works until near the end of the design cycle, start working on the guide now. Chances are you can muster support for doing so, since it has to be done eventually, but you will be able to do so in a way that forces the team to address some of the user-oriented issues.

Thinking about the documentation might help you to address user interface features that would otherwise have been delayed until later (probably too late to do anything user-based about them). Use some of the user-centered methods to come up with solutions to the problems—it's a somewhat sneaky but effective way to convince others of the importance of what you are doing.

Gain support through educating others

Expanding the process to include user-centered methodologies is really about expanding the outlooks of the people involved in the process. Not only will you have to be creative about incorporating these methods into the existing framework, but you will have to subtly tout the benefits of the techniques as you do so. This will help you educate others and gain support for the techniques in future design efforts.

Show people the effects of these methodologies on the quality of your software, and how you were able to solve design problems or come up with alternatives based on your work. If you are applying the methods in a way that they can improve the users' experiences, make sure to communicate users' positive responses. The most impressive way to do this is to have team members hear it from users themselves, either in person or on videotape. Showing how the people who will use the software think it is successful or not will lend solid support to your design methods. Point out why the methods you use make those responses possible. Your design teammates will see the value of these methods, and eventually the old framework will give way to a new one.

Seek out the user experts

Even if the existing process does not seem to support any user-centered design methodologies, chances are that somewhere in the framework there are ways that input from users is incorporated. Often it is not the design team that is responsible for understanding user needs; it gets information from other organizations with this function.

Typically, a marketing department is responsible for specifying user needs or requirements. If this is the case, seek out those responsible for providing this information. Talk to them about what they have learned from users and how they have done so. Ask for copies of any documents they have written or for results of any studies they have conducted. Analyze their findings according to the user-based techniques approach, re-evaluating the findings of the marketing experts, if necessary, to understand the impact on your design. In doing so, you might find a way in which different departments within your company can work together toward the same goals, and gain support for applying the user-centered approach to design.

Summary

What It All Means

Design is not a prescribed science, but an art relying on a range and knowledge of techniques, and knowing when to combine them. Interactive software design is greatly enhanced by involving the users of the software as, ultimately, the users determine the success or failure of a software product. The aesthetic quality of, or efficiency of the coding, is of little significance, if people cannot use the software for its intended task. People will use it if does what they need it to do, in a way that makes sense to them. In interactive software design, it is best to involve users as much as possible to insure their satisfaction with the final design.

The Role of Users in Software Design

In an ideal software design project, the development process starts with the users themselves, either by researching an existing system, technology or meeting with users. By interviewing users, the software developer can learn about current approaches, users' intended actions, and any limitations in existing software. Starting a design project by interacting with users can help guide it to meet user needs, rather than deliver a specific technology or haphazardly add new capabilities to an existing one. Even if the actual users of the target software are not available for direct observation , research can be conducted by interviewing designated "experts" or meeting with users of parallel technologies.

Involving users in software design should in no way be limited to the initial stages of design. Users can provide valuable input throughout the development of the project. There are ways to get users involved no matter the stage of design, the time, or budget available. These ways range from informally talking with, or observing, users and developing different kinds of prototypes; to showing designs to users and obtaining feedback; to conducting formal usability testing, and making recommendations based on statistical analysis of data gathered. When designing software, it is important to assess how user involvement can be most beneficial to a particular design and plan to include users in the development process. Scheduling time to observe users interacting with a system or application, dedicating energy to show prototypes, or allocating sessions for usability testing before the design is complete, can help to secure users' roles in software development.

User Interface Design Methods

A number of methods for involving users in the software design process are presented in the preceding chapters. These methods can be broken into the following categories:

Early User Research, Off-line Procedures, On-line

Procedures, Prototyping, Usability Testing and Iteration. Each type of user-oriented design methodology has its own considerations, including the importance and advantages of any particular method. While not all software designs require, or will be able to draw on, each of these types of methods, using any of these in the development of interactive software will enhance the software. This is true because each approach incorporates user needs or expectations. Determining the methods that are appropriate for a particular software project depends on the project, the nature of the software being developed, and the overall time frame of the project. Different projects will almost always employ different combinations of the techniques.

Project needs are not the only factor in determining which of the methods to put into place. Access to resources, or skill sets, will make certain of these methods easier. Having experience or training in graphic design, for instance, will help achieve high quality results in many of the off-line techniques, however, such expertise is not necessary to achieve adequate results which can make a significant difference in software design. Understanding the value of the various methods and knowing when to use them as intermediate steps can help to develop more complete and appropriate user interfaces. Anyone, even someone with no prior experience, can apply any of these methods to achieve worthwhile results. Clearly more expertise may help in the aesthetic quality of a prototype, or the degree of information gathered from users, but expertise can come with time. Any application of these procedures will enable user input to be gathered and some user input is infinitely better than none.

The accessibility of users is another important factor in determining which of these methods to apply on a given design . If users are readily available and currently using software, then early research or testing can make a lot of sense. However, if your users are inaccessible, say for potential security problems, focus your energy on prototyping (though you should at least try to get representative users to obtain some feedback in informal usability testing). Knowing how many users are available to you will decide how important user feedback can be in determining successive design steps. While input from one user is better than from none at all, you must take into account that without a representative user group you may not be gathering data that applies to all your potential users. Being aware, up front, of your capabilities and limitations can help better direct your design.

Altogether, the methods presented in preceding chapters can be used as steps in iterating a design. Iteration is a critical part of involving users in design, primarily because the nature of iteration is such that there are multiple generations of a design. A logical opportunity for user input is provided between design steps or cycles. Iteration can be used to refer to complete design phases, or merely the development steps created with successive applications of different techniques. A more complete, cycle-based iteration might start with user research; then involve some creative design and implementation; be shown to users to obtain feedback, and then incorporate this feedback in ensuing designs. This design-build-test cycle would continue until the design is complete (or resources are depleted, which is most often the determinant factor in design completion). A less complete iteration might involve the same stages but just one complete research-design-build-test loop. While this is not the most opportune way to incorporate user input, it at least acknowledges the importance of the user in software design and is often the only approach possible in design projects with limited budgets or resources.

Applying and Adapting Software Design Methods

The collection of methods presented here are not intended to be absolute. They are an informal set of techniques which can and should be adapted to the needs of an individual project or developer. Considerations such as the nature of the project, the time and resources available, and the composition of the design team can all play a role in determining how to best utilize these methods. Some of the techniques might work well in other (not computer software) design projects. Techniques may be adapted according to similar approaches you have found in other fields of research or development, such as customer research tactics followed by market research groups. The most important underlying factor in all the techniques is that they try to apply something about users - their preferences, their customs, their expectations - to the user interface under development. If only subsets of the methods, or different methods you have discovered elsewhere, work for a particular project, then by all means use those methods. Much of the creative application of these methods comes in knowing how and when to (or not to) apply them.

Likewise, any of these methods might be expanded to meet your own particular demands. These techniques can be used as a starting point to pursue more in-depth user research, or as the basis for more complex designs. Build on these steps to find the best way to involve users in your designs. You may discover or create alternate techniques that work better for you. The ability to introduce new techniques which incorporate user input in a creative or novel way is an indication of an understanding of the importance of user-based software design. As you become a more advanced user interface designer, you will become more adept at creating and adapting design methodologies.

General Steps for Software Design

In general, for most projects, you will want to take these overall steps:

1. Assess your project and time frame.
Understand the needs of this project, how you will take advantage of existing technology or develop new technologies. Do you know exactly what you will be building, or will it be tempered by early input from your users? Decide if you will be working toward a specific deadline, and if not what criteria will determine project completion.

2. Understand resources available to you.
Identify who will be working on your software design, their skills and available time, equipment and other materials, and overall budget. Knowing your capabilities and limitations can help direct your design.

3. Review existing experience.
Know which members of your team have completed similar projects, worked with one another, or dealt with comparable user populations. Understand

which methods team members have used in the past and why they were or were not effective.

4. Identify the users of your software and their accessibility.

Think about the range of people who will use your software and how they might be available to work with you in your design development. Ask yourself questions such as: Do you have ready access to your users? Can you share the technology with them? How agreeable will they be to working with you on your design?

5. Consider using experts, particularly if your users are not available.

Think about whether your users are well known by others, or whether your technology needs further exploration before pursuing the design. Seek out experts who can help set a foundation upon which you can build your design.

6. Select methods to be used.

Assess your project, resources, experience, users and experts to understand which user interface design methods make the most sense for your project. If you have more time and resources, you will probably want to encompass more of the techniques in your overall design. If you are limited, try to be more structured about identifying which methods are most appropriate. Remember that you can always add or remove certain steps as project needs change, but start with your ideal plan given what you know about your project.

7. Schedule the design and allocate resources.

Understand the total time you will need to devote to each method to enable you to complete your design in time. Determine who on your team will focus on which methods, and how they will work together to insure smooth integration of the design.

8. Plan to document your development as you go (with video tape or notes).

Keeping track of your design progress will help you be more thorough in your design as well as serve as a reference for later work.

9. Conduct each development step, with as many iterations as possible.

Finally, you are ready to tackle your design! Try not to accomplish everything in one design-build-test cycle - rather, start with big concepts and refine them on successive design-build-test iterations.

10. Make changes along the way if necessary.

Recognize that the software design process must be flexible enough to accommodate changes in project goals, user accessibility, or any revised distribution of resources that may come about as a result of user input or project management. Making changes to your plan, either in terms of allocated time or total number of steps and methods applied, does not indicate failure, rather it shows an adaptability that in the long run will help you to deliver better designs.

11. Assess your results.

Take the time to evaluate both your design and the procedure you followed. Understanding how various methods worked for or against you can give you experience which will help you in your future design projects. Evaluate how you worked with users and what you learned from your efforts - start to think about what you will do the same or differently next time around.

At first these steps may seem extraneous to your basic design needs. Up front, constructive planning will help your design and in the long run save you time. Assessing your process after the fact will help you learn from your successes and failures. You may of course choose not to include all of these steps every time, or limit or expand on any of them. However, you will probably want to consider following this general approach with each software application or system you design.

Final Thoughts

Software design, like any design process, is not about finding the absolute and perfect solution to a problem. For any technology or task there are probably numerous approaches which may follow completely different designs. Your job in designing a software user interface is to find one solution that meets the needs of your users - one that allows them to accomplish tasks in a way that makes sense to them. Keep in mind that there will always be design alternatives that you might try which will approach your problem in a slightly different way. Your design process need not be an exhaustive search for the ultimate solution. When you find something that works, stick with it. If in the future your solution turns out not to be as complete as you had hoped, you can change it later—*if it ain't broke don't fix it.*

Your criteria for evaluating whether or not the design works should always come from your users. You don't ever want to become so wrapped up in the design that you are unable to stand back and see how the people who must use it to accomplish real tasks, feel about it. You may be the designer, but once you deliver the software your users will be the most impacted by the final design. Regard users as your allies in development - people who can help you learn what you need to know about your design - rather than as obstacles to getting your technology to work.

Most of all, having a range and a variety of techniques for user interface design should allow you to find an approach that works for you. If you are a people person, concentrate on methods that provide direct interaction with your users. If you like to explore design alternatives, direct more energy toward your off-line or on-line prototypes. At times you may need to choose methods that don't utilize your strongest skills for the sake of your current design. However, for the most part, you are justified in selecting methods at which you best excel or simply most enjoy. Take advantage of the range of software design methods and find your element of fun!

Bibliography

Apple Computer, Inc., **Macintosh Human Interface Guidelines.** Reading, MA: Addison-Wesley Publishing Company, 1992.

Bauersfeld, Penny and Gomoll, Kathleen, **User-Centered Prototyping.** Class notes for design classes offered in-house at various companies and organizations, 1993.

Bauersfeld, Penny, Gomoll, Kathleen and Vertelney, Laurie, **User-Oriented Interface Design.** Class notes for User-Oriented Interface Design: Process and Product, Short Course, UCLA Extension Program, September 1991, July 1992 and September 1993.

Gentner, Donald R and Grudin, Jonathan, **Why Good Engineers (Sometimes) Create Bad Interfaces,** in CHI'90 Conference Proceedings. Reading, MA: Addison-Wesley Company, Inc., 1990.

Gomoll, Kathleen, **Some Techniques for Observing Users** from The Art of Human-Computer Interface Design, Brenda Laurel, editor. Reading, MA: Addison-Wesley Publishing Company, Inc., 1990.

Goodman, Danny, **The Complete HyperCard 2.0 Handbook.** Toronto, CN: Bantam Books, 1990.

Mountford, S.J., Vertelney, L., Bauersfeld, P., Gomoll, K. and Tognazzini, B., **Designers: Meet Your Users,** panel session from CHI'90 Conference Proceedings. Reading, MA: Addison-Wesley Company, Inc., 1990.

Norman, Donald A., **Design of Everyday Things** (formerly Psychology of Everyday Things). New York: Basic Books, Inc, Publishers, 1988.

Salomon, Gitta B, **Designing Casual-Use Hypertext: The CHI'89 InfoBooth,** in CHI'90 Conference Proceedings. Reading, MA: Addison-Wesley Company, Inc., 1990.

Vertelney, Laurie, **Using Video to Prototype User Interfaces,** in SIGCHI Bulletin, October 1980, Volume 21, Number 2.

Wurman, Richard S., **Information Anxiety: What to Do When Information Doesn't Tell You What You Need to Know.** New York: Bantam Books, 1990.

Index

off-line flipbooks vs., 147, 149
  steps for building, 151-152
  using, 149-150
On-line tools and procedures, 109-153.
    See also Early on-line
    explorations
  advantages of, 112-113
  backbone, creating system, 134-139
  clip art, 139-147
  definition of, 109
  for drawing, 85
  early user studies, incorporation of,
    115-116
  flipbooks, on-line, 147-153
  obtaining user feedback from, 111
  and off-line designs, 111, 114
  platforms for, 110-111
  steps for selecting, designing and
    performing, 113-117
  system requirements, 124-133
  timing factors, 109-110, 114

P

Partial systems, performing usability
    tests on, 200
Patterns of user behavior, identification
    of, in early user studies, 32
Planning and scheduling (of prototypes),
    164-170
  basic components of, 165
  hints and suggestions for, 169-170
  for home library (example), 166-167
  importance of, 167-168
  iteration, planning for, 246,
    250-251, 253
  steps for, 169
  time factors in, 165, 169
Platforms

for early on-line explorations,
    120-121
  and on-line flipbooks, 151
  for on-line tools and procedures,
    110-111
Portable device, flipbook for, 101
Product design, 8-9
Programming language
  system backbone and, 136, 138
  and tool selection, 175
  using software prototyping tools
    instead of, 179
Prototypes
  on-line, 110-111, 114-117
  testing technology capabilities
    with, 29
  use of, 163
Prototyping, 155-191. *See also* Software
    prototyping tool(s)
  advantages of, 158-160
  deciding on approach for, 157-158
  definition of, 155-156
  expendability and, 156
  and final software, 162
  goals of, 156-157
  and iterative design, 156, 159-160
  past experience, integrating, 164
  planning and scheduling, 160-161,
    164-170
  rapid, 156
  resources for, 161
  steps for selecting, designing and
    performing, 160-164
  timing factors, 158
  tool selection for, 170-177
  and transition to actual software,
    190-191
  and use of prototypes, 163
  and user access, 163